ROMAN LONDON

BY THE SAME AUTHOR:

The Roman City of London

ROMAN LONDON

Ralph Merrifield

FREDERICK A. PRAEGER, *Publishers*
New York · Washington

BOOKS THAT MATTER
Published in the United States of America in 1969
by Frederick A. Praeger, Inc., Publishers
111 Fourth Avenue, New York, N.Y. 10003

Library of Congress Catalog Card Number: 75-75111

Printed in Great Britain

TO MY MOTHER

Contents

Illustrations

Acknowledgments

As this book is necessarily the compendium of the work of many people, past and present, who have sought to extend our knowledge of Roman London, thanks are due first to these. Special mention must be made of those who have laboured mightily in this field to take advantage of the special opportunities that have arisen since the war: Professor W. F. Grimes and the Roman and Mediaeval London Excavation Council; my colleagues in Guildhall Museum, past and present, and especially Messrs Norman Cook, I. Noël Hume and Peter Marsden; the active amateur excavators of the City of London Archaeological Society and the Southwark and Lambeth Archaeological Society. Thanks are especially due to those who have generously made the results of their investigations available in advance of the publication of their own reports: Messrs J. Ashdown, G. Beeby, V. F. Bignell, A. Brown, F. Celoria, N. Farrant, D. Imber, B. Philp and H. Sheldon. I am also very grateful to the following for reading certain sections of this book and for making helpful suggestions, which have mostly been adopted: Messrs V. F. Bignell, R. Canham, M. Henig, P. R. V. Marsden, I. D. Margary and D. J. Turner. Assistance was also received in various special fields from Miss J. M. C. Toynbee, Professor Sheppard Frere, Dr J. P. C. Kent, Dr J. Morris, Mr K. S. Painter, Dr Graham Webster and Mr R. P. Wright.

Acknowledgment must also be made to the following for kindly supplying photographs and permitting them to be used: the British Museum, the London Museum, Guildhall Museum, the Press Association and Mr Brian Philp; and to Mr R. P. Wright for permitting reproduction from *The Roman Inscriptions of Britain*. I am also very grateful to Mr Alan Sorrell for his excellent new reconstruction of Roman London.

Writing a book as a spare-time activity requires considerable forbearance from those who have to live with the author, and special gratitude would have been due for this alone to my wife. As she has also cheerfully shouldered the duties of secretary, cartographer, literary adviser and indexer, her part in the production of this book does not fall far short of co-authorship.

BIBLIOGRAPHY AND ABBREVIATIONS

A. Birley. *Life in Roman Britain*, 1964

R. L. S. Bruce-Mitford (ed.). *Recent Archaeological Excavations in Britain*, 1956

R. G. Collingwood and R. P. Wright. *The Roman Inscriptions of Britain*, Vol. I, 1965 (*RIB*)

F. Cumont. *Oriental Religions in Roman Paganism*, 1956

S. S. Frere. *Britannia. A History of Roman Britain*, 1967 (*Britannia*)

* W. F. Grimes. *The Excavation of Roman and Mediaeval London*, 1968

E. & J. R. Harris. *The Oriental Cults in Roman Britain*, 1965

K. M. Kenyon. *Excavations in Southwark*, 1959

I. D. Margary. *Roman Roads in Britain*. 2nd ed., 1967 (*RRB*)

I. D. Margary. *Roman Ways in the Weald*, 1948

P. R. V. Marsden. *A Roman Ship from Blackfriars, London*. Guildhall Museum Publication

R. Merrifield. *The Roman City of London*, 1965 (*RCL*)

J. E. Price. *On a Bastion of London Wall*, 1880

C. Roach Smith. *Illustrations of Roman London*, 1859 (*IRL*)

Royal Commission on Historical Monuments. *An Inventory of the Historical Monuments in London*. Vol. III. *Roman London* (*RCHM : RL*)

Royal Commission on Historical Monuments. *South-East Essex* (*RCHM : SE Essex*)

J. Stow. *A Survey of London* (Kingsford Edition)

J. M. C. Toynbee. *Art in Britain under the Romans*, 1964

J. M. C. Toynbee. *Art in Roman Britain*, 1962

The Viatores. *Roman Roads in the South-East Midlands*, 1964

R. E. M. Wheeler. *London in Roman Times*. London Museum Catalogue No. 3, 1930 (*London in R. Times*)

C. Wren. *Parentalia, or Memoirs of the Family of the Wrens*, 1750

* Professor Grimes's book unfortunately appeared too late to be used in the preparation of this work, but is included in the Bibliography because of its great importance to the student of Roman London.

PERIODICALS

Antiquaries Journal (Ant. Journ.)
Archaeologia (Arch.)
Archaeologia Cantiana (Arch. Cant.)
Archaeological Journal (Arch. Journ.)
Journal of the British Archaeological Association (JBAA)
Journal of Roman Studies (JRS)
London and Middlesex Archaeological Society Transactions (LAMAS Trans.)
Proceedings of the Society of Antiquaries of London (Proc. Soc. Ant.)

Buried London

The fragments that remain of the Roman city of Londinium lie buried deep beneath the pavements and the shallower cellars of the modern City, and the original ground-surface on which the earliest Londoners walked, where it survives, lies mostly between ten and twenty feet below the present street-level. The gradual accumulation of man-made ground above this has been made by the same process that created the artificial hills called *tells*, which mark the sites of ancient cities in the east. Durable materials have been brought from outside and used to construct buildings that eventually fell into decay, or became obsolete and were pulled down; not infrequently they came to a premature end in one of the many fires that have devastated London. Then the ruins of the old building were levelled but not removed, and its successor rose on the same site, with its floors at a slightly higher level. This process, continued for nineteen centuries, has been the principal cause of the rise in the ground-level, but there have been other contributing factors. One of these has been the steady accumulation of human waste—the discarded refuse of a closely concentrated community. Week after week, year after year, food, clothing, household equipment and other consumer goods have poured into London—and have remained as organic waste, bones and pot-sherds to contribute to its vertical growth. The removal of such refuse outside the city is a very recent development, and until the early nineteenth century the London householder could only bury it, usually on his own premises. A more important factor in the low-lying areas of the city has been due to major geographical changes that have taken place since Roman times. A gradual sinking of the land-mass of south-

I

east Britain has resulted in the steady rise of the water-level relative to the land, so that the tides, which barely reached the site of the Roman city in the early years of the occupation, now extend as far as Teddington, twenty-one miles farther upstream. At high spring-tide the water-level at London Bridge is therefore now about thirteen feet above its level when the first Roman bridge was built. As a result of the gradual rise in the relative water-level, the tributaries of the Thames in this area became sluggish, with an increasing tendency to silt up and to flood their banks. One of these, later called the Walbrook, flowed through the heart of Roman London, and in its valley occupation could be maintained only by dumping earth on the flooded banks to raise the ground-level above the water. It was necessary to repeat this process periodically as the flood-waters rose ever higher, until eventually the whole valley was practically filled, partly by flood-silt but mostly by material deliberately dumped there by man. It is in the middle of the Walbrook valley that there is the greatest difference (more than thirty feet) between the original level and that of the present day. On the top of Cornhill the depth of the accumulation is about seventeen feet, and on the higher ground west of the Walbrook valley, in the neighbourhood of St Paul's Cathedral, it is only thirteen feet. Since the rise of London's ground-level has been greatest in the low-lying areas, its effect has been to level the ground rather than to produce an artificial hill. The edges of the city's *tell* have in fact been masked by a similar accumulation outside, since refuse was deposited round the perimeter of the town at an early date, and later the spread of buildings beyond the city walls affected a wider area in a similar way.

Here also the rising waters played their part. To the north, Moorfields became a marsh in which peat grew, until the district was reclaimed in the sixteenth century by raising the ground-level artificially; to the south, the tides rose ever higher, engulfing more and more of the city mound, the true height of which can only be appreciated from the river at its lowest ebb.

When we stand in the City of London, the debris of the past lies beneath our feet in stratified layers, with the earliest remains of the Roman city of Londinium at the bottom, immediately above the original soil-level. Unfortunately for the archaeologist, these layers are not only inaccessible beneath pavements and office cellars under ordinary circumstances, but in most places survive intact only in small areas. They are pierced and intersected by holes and channels dug through them in all the subsequent periods of occupation, so that a single Roman floor may be broken by a later Roman foundation, a medieval well, a seventeenth-century cellar and a nineteenth-century drain. Our knowledge of Roman London has been mostly built up by observation of such fragments, as they have come to light in excavations for buildings and sewers. Under these circumstances it is rarely possible to recover sufficient of the plan of an ancient building for its purpose and character to be identified with certainty. Scraps of dating evidence may be found, usually in the form of pottery sherds from deposits that antedate the structure or that have accumulated after its demolition, but it is only in comparatively recent times that much attention has been given to these. Roman walls and pavements have been noted with interest by antiquaries, as they came to light, for more than three hundred years, but their precise position was seldom recorded before the latter part of the nineteenth century, and it has been left to archaeologists of the present century to attempt to define their date within the Roman period—which lasted a little longer than the time between the reigns of Queen Elizabeth I and II. With the best will and the most efficient technique, however, it is impossible to unravel satisfactorily the complex stratification of a City site merely by watching or enlarging a builder's excavation. It can only be done by meticulous and skilful archaeological excavation, in which the various structures and deposits are carefully removed in the reverse order to that in which they had accumulated, so that at any phase in the work the latest that remains will be the next to be taken out, whether it be the foundation of a wall or the filling of a deep pit. Each must be conscientiously recorded and all dating evidence saved for further study. All this requires skilled direction and labour, some money, and above all *time*. The greatest handicap to archaeological research in the City of London is in fact the high value of the land, which makes any delay in restoring it to full productiveness as a source of income very costly to its owner. Under normal circumstances, therefore, demolition of an old building is immediately followed by the construction of the new.

The destruction of a large part of the City by German bombs at the end of 1940 and the beginning of 1941, however, gave archaeologists an exceptional opportunity in the years immediately following the war. Many acres lay devastated, and the process of reconstruction was necessarily slow, so that for the first time since the development of modern archaeological technique it could be

3

applied to the complex problems of London's early history. On the initiative of the Council for British Archaeology and the Society of Antiquaries of London, the Roman and Mediaeval London Excavation Council was set up to take advantage of this situation. The Council was fortunate in obtaining the services of W. F. Grimes, one of our most experienced excavators, as its Director of Excavations. Time, opportunity and skilled direction were now available; labour could be trained; a fifth essential—sufficient money —was always lacking. The Ministry of Works (as it was then called) made an annual grant that was generous in proportion to the total funds available to it for subsidizing similar work throughout the country; other organizations and individuals made modest donations, but sufficient support to make possible an all-out campaign of excavation on a large scale was never forthcoming.

On nearly every site, before archaeological excavation could begin, it was necessary to clear away the rubble of the bombed building and to break up the concrete basement below it. Unproductive work of this kind took up a great deal of the time of the Council's few workmen, so that the areas that could be investigated were very limited. Nevertheless, some scientific excavation was carried out in all parts of the City that had been devastated, and the precisely recorded sections that were obtained will be of the greatest value to future students. This work was especially useful in demonstrating the presence of the humbler buildings of Roman London, constructed with timber frames and with walls of wattle and daub, which can seldom be observed in the conditions of a builders' excavation.

The deployment of such a small force in the face of an almost limitless task demanded generalship of a high order, with a careful planning of cuttings where the maximum of results could be expected for the minimum of unproductive labour. Since area excavations seemed impossible, the efforts of the Excavation Council in investigating Roman London—and medieval London, with its lost churches and priories, was also demanding attention—were mainly concentrated on problems likely to be solved by selective sectioning. The most important of these was the history of the City's defences —and Professor Grimes's greatest discovery was the Roman fort that antedated the city wall. Another major investigation showed the true nature of the stream of the Walbrook, which previously had been completely misunderstood—and here an unexpected bonus was the finding of the temple of Mithras that stood upon its bank.

For the rest of the bombed city a policy of sampling was adopted, with results that were seldom spectacular, but that gave precise information for the first time about the early occupation and subsequent history of a few square yards in each area.

The rebuilding of the blitzed sites within the walls of Roman London has since been practically completed, but, as it proceeded, much more of the ancient city came briefly to light before its destruction by the jaws of the mechanical grab. Successive excavation assistants of Guildhall Museum, usually working single-handed, made heroic efforts to record as much as possible, always in difficult, and sometimes in dangerous conditions, before it disappeared for ever. On many sites where a post-war office block now stands, destruction has been complete, and all traces of ancient London have been removed to make way for the basements of the new building. In other instances, the new block may stand on foundations that penetrate deeply into the subsoil but do not cover the entire area of the site, so that pockets of archaeological deposits remain between them, completely inaccessible until the new offices are themselves destroyed, but offering some hope for further investigation by future generations. In the meantime every opportunity is being taken to observe builders' excavations as they occur, and to carry out controlled archaeological excavations in those areas that have remained open—temporary car-parks and the like.

I have elsewhere given a detailed account of the structures of Roman London recorded by archaeologists and others in the last three hundred years.[1] The present book is intended mainly as a guide to those who wish to see and understand the visible traces of the Roman city and its people.

Excavations are of brief duration and are often inaccessible, so that they can seldom be visited by the public. Moreover, the remains that they reveal are for the most part unimpressive in appearance and not easily understood even by the expert, until he has carefully worked out the complex sequence of structures that appear. Even then the surviving fragment of an ancient building may be of little significance until it is brought into relationship with other fragments that are no longer visible—and may even have been recorded and destroyed many years before. There have, of course, been exceptional cases in which the remains found have been so

[1] *The Roman City of London, 1965.*

5

B

complete or so impressive that they have attracted widespread interest—the temple of Mithras was such a case—but these are very rare indeed. The visitor will therefore seldom have an opportunity to study an excavation actually in progress, and will gain very little from it if he does.

A few of the more striking and interesting remains have, however, been preserved *in situ*, in open ground, in the basements of existing buildings, or in specially constructed cells, and most of these can be visited. Some can be seen at any time or at certain fixed hours, but others can be inspected only by special arrangement with the owners. In the latter group, permission to view is readily granted in some instances, if sufficient notice is given, but in others it is not always practicable or convenient to admit visitors. Tours of the visible remains of Roman London therefore require careful planning, which must be done well in advance if any of the less accessible sites are to be visited. Knowledge also is required—not only of the whereabouts and significance of the surviving remains, but also of the circumstances in which some of them can be visited. It is one of the purposes of this book to supply the necessary information, but it must be emphasized that where there is no public access the last word necessarily rests with the owner of the site, who, with the best will in the world, may find it quite impossible to reconcile the admission of visitors to view antiquities with the proper function of his building.

There is, however, another sense in which traces of Roman London still survive in the modern City. The 'Square Mile' that is the financial and commercial centre of Britain may now be a place of impersonal office blocks, interspersed with alleys and Wren churches that are the only obvious reminders of a more human past. The topography of the City has, however, been determined by its history, and this began when the invading Romans built the first London Bridge. The course of the Roman city wall can still be followed for much of its length, indicated by modern streets parallel with its line or, more closely, by modern walls that mark a property boundary determined by the position of the ancient wall. Busy thoroughfares break its line, and now, as in Roman times, give access to the city where the Roman gates stood at Aldgate, Bishopsgate, Aldersgate, Newgate and Ludgate. The present street-plan of the City within the walls is very different from what is known of the Roman street-plan, but certain modern streets still follow, at least in part, the lines that were laid out by the Romans.

They are clearly the direct descendants of their ancient predecessors that lie buried deeply beneath them. To this extent, then, Londinium is still visible to the informed explorer of the City. Even earlier features can be discerned in the contours of the present pavements and tarmac roads, sometimes distinctly and sometimes only very faintly. The long-lost streams, banks and hillocks that formed the natural scenery as it appeared to the invading armies of AD 43, can still be detected in the rise and fall of the modern surface that lies many feet above them. Norman barons, medieval friars, Tudor and Stuart entrepreneurs, railway engineers, speculative builders and modern town-planners have all contributed to the shape of the City as it appears today; and only the information given by archaeology makes it possible for us to trace the hand of the Roman in this confusion, and to appreciate the physical setting in which he built the first London. Although a guide must be primarily concerned with what is actually visible, this will make little sense except in the context of a wider knowledge of the topography of Roman London. An attempt will therefore be made to re-create this—at least in outline—in relation to the modern City; and the position, not only of streets and streams, but of some of the more important buildings, will be indicated, although nothing of them may now survive, even beneath the surface.

A city does not consist only of streets and buildings, however; and to give life to this long-vanished scene we must turn to something that can fortunately be seen without any difficulty. London has yielded an immense archaeological treasure, of which a great part has fortunately passed into public ownership and is therefore readily accessible. The kitchen- and table-ware of the Roman Londoners, the tools used in their trades, their personal ornaments, weapons and footwear have all survived in abundance. Even their ideas and beliefs remain, embodied in works of art of high and low degree. Some of these citizens we know by name, and in a surprising number of instances they are able to speak directly to us in their own words: in letters, *graffiti* and inscriptions, they speak of commercial transactions, of their devotion to their gods, of hatred of their enemies, of the grief of bereavement—and of the merely trivial.

These things can all be seen in the three museums that possess important collections of antiquities from Roman London—the British Museum, the London Museum and Guildhall Museum. The two last, at present housed respectively in Kensington Palace

7

and in temporary quarters north of Guildhall,[1] are to be united in a new Museum of London which, it is hoped, will be built before many more years have passed, in Aldersgate Street, about five hundred yards north of St Paul's. In the fine new building that has already been planned, it will one day be possible to see the subject of Roman London, and all the other chapters of London's history, worthily illustrated by a really great collection, on a site that looks to the east on the historic walled city with its medieval bastions, to the south on Wren's magnificent cathedral, and to the north on the exciting new development of Barbican.

Since the present unsatisfactory accommodation of the London and Guildhall Museums is, it is hoped, merely temporary, and since the arrangement of the gallery of Romano-British antiquities at the British Museum is not yet final, no guide to the existing arrangements will be given. Instead, the three collections will be discussed together, in relation to the light that they throw collectively on the various aspects of life in Roman London. The museum in which the more important individual antiquities are to be found will, however, be indicated.

In addition to the three main collections, reference will also be made to the more important antiquities from Roman London in the private museums of various London institutions. These are not open to the public under ordinary conditions, but can sometimes be visited by special arrangement, through the favour of their owners.

There are also a few local collections of Romano-British antiquities found in the Greater London area, which are housed in various museums and libraries. These reflect not the life of Londinium itself—except in so far as they contain stray material from the City—but that of outlying settlements in the surrounding countryside. One, however, is of especial importance, both for its extent and for its close connexion with the Roman city. This belongs to the Cuming Museum in Southwark, and contains material from the southern suburb of Londinium, which grew up very early at the south end of the Roman bridge, and subsequently extended in a line of ribbon development along Stane Street.

Roads, for the most part still in use, are almost the only visible legacy of the Romans in London outside the City, but the practice of burying the dead by the wayside, outside the inhabited area, has

[1] In converted shop-premises on the Bassishaw High Walk, with offices in Gillett House, 55 Basinghall Street, E.C.2.

8

resulted in occasional discoveries of urns, coffins and even inscriptions, at considerable distances from the Roman city and its
southern suburb. The nearer burials are no doubt merely outliers
of the great extra-mural cemeteries of the Roman city, but those
that are more remote must indicate the existence of a rural population in the London area, e.g. in Bow and East Ham, Hackney,
Holborn, Westminster, Battersea, Putney, Southwark, Blackheath,
Woolwich and Plumstead. Here there were no doubt farmsteads
that helped to supply Londinium with its food, but as yet we know
very little about them.

It is the purpose of the present book to give a general account of
Roman London in its various aspects, relating this as closely as
possible to what is visible today, as topographical survivals on the
surface, as fragments of buildings preserved below ground-level,
or as antiquities in the show-cases of museums. Readers requiring
more details of past discoveries are referred to Professor Grimes's
The Excavation of Roman and Mediaeval London, published in 1968,
for an excellent account of the work of the Roman and Mediaeval
London Excavation Council in the twenty years of intensive
archaeological investigation that followed the end of the last war;
and to my own *Roman City of London*, published in 1965, for
summaries of the work done by Guildhall Museum in the same
period, and of all earlier discoveries. To keep up to date with more
recent finds, reference should be made to the brief summaries that
appear each year in the *Journal of Roman Studies*, and to the fuller
reports that are subsequently published in the *London and Middlesex
Archaeological Society Transactions*.

CHAPTER ONE

The Origin of London

It now requires a great deal of imagination to visualize the London area as it was before the coming of the Romans. Not only must we sweep away all the streets and buildings, with the accumulated man-made layers beneath them, leaving the landscape more sharply contoured, but we must also restore the natural vegetation, which was determined mainly by the nature of the subsoil. Over most of the London region is the characteristic London Clay, bluish-grey in colour at a depth, but brownish where it lies near the surface. Overlying this in the Thames valley are three gravel terraces, which have been of the greatest importance in determining human occupation until modern times. Central London is built on the two lower terraces, the Middle Terrace forming the two gravel 'hills' (actually plateaux) of the City and the higher ground of the West End. In many places the gravel is overlaid by brick-earth, a brown, clay-like loam deposited as sludge during the Ice Age. Much less impervious than the London Clay, it still tends to retain the water for a time after heavy rain. Finally in the present valleys of the Thames and its tributaries is a more recent deposit of alluvial silt.

When the Romans came to Britain, the London Clay surface was covered by oak forest with a dense undergrowth of hazel, hawthorn and brambles, such as may still be seen in Epping Forest, twelve miles to the north-east of the City. This thick jungle enclosed the London area to the north, broken only by patches of heathland where a sandy surface occurred—as at Hampstead, Highgate and Harrow. Much more open country was to be seen on the gravels nearer the river, although these might be lightly wooded, especially where they were overlaid by brick-earth. In general, however, they would probably have supported light scrub with occasional trees. In the wet alluvial soil beside the river and its tributary streams there would have been thickets of alder and willow. South of the Thames the thickly-wooded claylands were less continuous, being broken at intervals by the scrubland and heaths of the more extensive gravels and sands.

The Thames had served as a great waterway into Britain throughout prehistory, and settlers were attracted to the more open country on its banks, especially in those places where the river could be crossed by fords. The abundance of finds of the later prehistoric periods in the Thames at Brentford indicates that this was one of the favoured areas, and it is suspected that there was a settlement of importance in the neighbourhood. The water was then at least twelve feet lower than the present high-water-level, and the river would have been much narrower at this point, so that it could have been forded quite easily. Open country, suitable for primitive farming, lay on both banks, and also to the north and west, where the stream of the Brent provided a convenient water-supply. Similarly, a short distance up the river, another tributary, the Crane, flowed through open heathland at Hounslow, and here again important finds of the Bronze and Early Iron Ages have occurred. The number of interesting discoveries in the river at Barnes, Hammersmith, Fulham, Wandsworth, Chelsea and Battersea indicates that there was pre-Roman occupation of the Thames-side gravels upstream of Westminster, but we know nothing of the settlements themselves.

Our only clear picture of an Early Iron Age settlement on the gravels of the London region comes from much farther west, on the site of London Airport at Heathrow. Here, near a small feeder of the Colne, itself a tributary of the Thames, was a small earthwork popularly known as 'Caesar's Camp'. This was excavated by Professor W. F. Grimes, and found to be a village, or rather hamlet, which was occupied from an early period of the Early Iron Age. (*Fig. 1*.) It was a quadrangular enclosure, about 125 yards across, defended by a ditch and a bank. The southern part of the enclosure was empty, but in the northern part had been a cluster of eleven circular wooden huts, no doubt with thatched roofs, not unlike those of a modern African village. It is clear that this was not merely a farmstead, but a community consisting of several families. To the south of the huts on the western side was a rectangular temple, consisting of a central shrine surrounded by a colonnade of posts,

Fig. 1 *Reconstruction of the Heathrow
Early Iron Age hamlet by Alan Sorrell*

very much like a translation into wood and thatch of the stone-built
Greek temples of the Mediterranean. With overall dimensions of
about 36 by 32 feet, this was the dominant building of the enclosure, and the one unusual feature of what would otherwise have
been a fairly typical settlement of the later prehistoric period. The
temple continued in use for a long period, and may well have served
the religious needs of a much larger population than the inhabitants
of the Heathrow hamlet.[1] If so, we may suspect that scattered
through the neighbouring countryside were similar small farming
communities—and quite certainly isolated farms as well—linked by
kinship, religion and trade, but with little sense of political unity
beyond a tendency to co-operate briefly in self-defence in the face
of a common danger.

[1] *Archaeology*, I (1948), pp. 74–8; S. S. Frere (ed.): *Problems of the Iron Age in Southern Britain*,
p. 25.

Traces of a stronghold constructed on such an occasion can still be seen on Wimbledon Common, where it occupies a high position above the Thames valley. It is roughly circular, and consists of a single rampart and ditch, forming a ring about three hundred yards in diameter. Unfortunately, the site is leased to the Royal Wimbledon Golf Club, and access to the public is limited to a narrow path through the middle, from which only part of the half-obliterated bank and ditch can be seen. Although it is called 'Caesar's Camp', like the earthwork at Heathrow (which dates from about 400 BC), it was probably constructed more than two hundred years before the invasion of Julius Caesar.[1] Hill-forts of this kind were occupied only briefly by a force sufficient to defend them, and that must have been drawn from a considerable area of the surrounding countryside.

Large permanent congregations of population could not be supported by the economy, and were in any case alien to Celtic society, which probably found all the opportunities it required for commerce, courtship and entertainment in seasonal religious gatherings. We need not therefore look for a tribal centre as the precursor of London. Even in the first century BC, when tribal capitals did develop, after the political and military abilities of the Belgae had imposed the rule of their princes over south-eastern Britain, these were well away from the Thames—though accessible from it—in strongholds partly encircled by woodland at such places as Wheathampstead, and later at St Albans, Silchester and Colchester. The river itself served as a frontier between the tribal kingdoms as well as a means of communication, and its banks were therefore too peripheral and too exposed to provide a convenient and secure site for the capital of a Belgic warrior chief.

In the absence of any archaeological or historical evidence to the contrary—and in spite of the persistent legend of a pre-Roman London—it must therefore be assumed that the London area was occupied before the Roman conquest by only a scattered rural population in units no larger than a small village, gaining its living mainly by mixed farming, supplemented to some extent by fishing. It is doubtful whether there was even a small community of this kind on the site of Roman Londinium, which later became the City of London. Comparatively few prehistoric objects have been found in the City, and most of these are of the kind that could have been

---

[1] *Arch. Journ.*, CII (1947), pp. 15–20, where a date in the 3rd century BC is attributed to the pottery from the Wimbledon earthwork.

accidentally lost by casual visitors. A certain proportion of them may even have been found elsewhere and taken there as curiosities or magical charms by Londoners, long after the period of their manufacture. The extensive archaeological investigations that have now been carried out in many parts of the City have revealed no evidence of any actual settlement in pre-Roman times. Only a few sherds of Bronze Age pottery testified to the presence of people of that period in the Cripplegate area, but the indication was of the slightest possible occupation—that of a temporary resting-place rather than of a permanent home. In the case of the pre-Roman Iron Age, there is as yet no evidence of any actual occupation in the City at all. The very few antiquities that can definitely be attributed to this period might easily have been still in use after the founding of Londinium in the mid-first century AD. Some kinds of personal possession could survive in use for a long time as family heirlooms, as is perhaps exemplified by the fine 'anthropoid' dagger—so called because its hilt is in the form of a human figure—found in Stoney Street, Southwark, and now in Guildhall Museum. (*Fig. 2*.) This

Fig. 2 *Pre-Roman (Early Iron Age) iron dagger from Stoney Street, Southwark*

is a weapon that can hardly have been made later than the first century BC, but it was found apparently associated with two vases and a trident of Roman date. (The association is doubtful, however, since all four objects may be from a riverine deposit.) The same explanation would account for the occasional discoveries of fine imported Italian (Arretine) pottery of pre-conquest date in the City and Southwark.[1] This ware was acquired through trade by the Belgic aristocrats of Calleva (Silchester), Verulamium (St Albans) and Camulodunum (Colchester) in the reigns of Augustus, Tiberius

[1] *RCHM: RL*, pp. 24–7, 179–81.

and Caligula, and may well have been brought by themselves or by their sons to Londinium in its early years. Fine ware of this kind, like the later Gaulish red-gloss pottery, which was often carefully repaired after damage, was valued and therefore likely to continue in use for a long period. Its scattered occurrence from Southwark to Bishopsgate cannot be regarded as evidence for a settlement in the City area either of Britons or foreign traders before the Claudian conquest.

Julius Caesar passed through the London region in 54 BC, but makes no reference to any large settlement on the banks of the Thames, though no doubt he saw here some of the many homesteads 'like those of the Gauls', which he says were so numerous in Britain. The place where he crossed the river into the territory of Cassivellaunus is unknown, but certain deductions can be made from his account, set against the general topographical and archaeological background of the area. He says that the river was fordable at one point only, and even there with difficulty. At this place large enemy forces were drawn up on the opposite bank, which was fenced by large stakes fixed along the edge, and he was told by prisoners and deserters that similar ones were concealed in the river-bed. Nevertheless, he delivered a frontal attack with both cavalry and infantry, who had only their heads above water. The defending British force was overpowered and fled from the bank. Cassivellaunus now made skilful use of the thick woodlands that lay to the north of the Thames, hiding in them the cattle that would have been seized for food by the invading army, and ambushing the Roman cavalry from them with his chariots if it ventured far from the main column of infantry. The Belgae, true to their Germanic origin, were at home in the forest, and were familiar with lanes and pathways through it, from which their attacks could be launched. While the Romans continued their difficult trek into the interior, they were contacted by envoys from the Trinovantes, the tribe that occupied Essex and Suffolk, offering to surrender and asking for protection against Cassivellaunus. Caesar demanded hostages and supplies of grain, which were promptly sent. Five other tribes—the Cenimagni, Segontiaci, Ancalites, Bibroci and Cassi—followed the example of the Trinovantes and surrendered. We do not know the territories of these people, but they were presumably minor tribes of the Thames basin, who had been dominated by Cassivellaunus. They now betrayed their overlord and directed Caesar to his secret stronghold, which was quite near.

15

This was protected by forest and marsh, and had been strongly fortified, but was unable to withstand the assault of the legions, although most of the defenders were able to escape. Later, after the failure of an attack on the Roman naval base in Kent, Cassivellaunus sued for peace.[1]

The point at which Caesar crossed the Thames has been the subject of conjecture for centuries, and the places that have been suggested range from Coway Stakes, near Walton, to Westminster. The stakes at Coway ran across the stream and were clearly not defensive, but may have been the remains of fishing weirs;[2] those at Brentford were in lines parallel with the bank, but may be of any date, and could be the remains of a revetted embankment. Some are said to have been sharpened and pointing outward at an angle of 45°,[3] but in the absence of a more precise record, we cannot be sure that these were not cross-ties of the revetment. The problem of the Brentford stakes is clearly worth further investigation if an opportunity arises, and a Carbon 14 test could presumably establish the age of the wood. It would be necessary to be quite certain, however, that the stake tested was one of a series in line parallel with the bank, for ancient piles that supported dwellings are common in this area.

Chelsea has been claimed as Caesar's crossing-place on the strength of finds made when Chelsea Bridge was built in 1854–5. A number of weapons were found, and also human skulls, said to be 'of two distinct types—British and Roman', mainly between the Middlesex bank and midstream.[4] Unfortunately the weapons from the river here are of many different dates. The 'spear-head' recorded by Syer Cuming, who suggested this as the site of a battle between Britons and Romans, was in fact a poniard of the Middle Bronze Age; while the skulls that he attributed so confidently to the two opposing armies he did not see at all, identifying his two types from 'exceedingly rude' drawings that he was shown! They could of course be of any date, and were probably of more than one period like the weapons.

One warlike object from this part of the river, that is at least of the right century, is the magnificent decorated bronze shield that was found nearer the Battersea side, and is one of the greatest treasures of the British Museum. (*Fig. 3.*) It belongs to the latest phase of

[1] Caesar: *De Bello Gallico*, V, 18–22.
[2] *Arch.*, II, p. 144.
[3] C. E. Vulliamy: *The Archaeology of Middlesex and London*, pp. 279–80.
[4] *JBAA*, XIII (1857), pp. 237–40.

Fig. 4 *Pre-Roman* (*Early Iron Age*) *bronze helmet, probably 1st century* BC, *from the Thames at Waterloo Bridge*

Fig. 3 *Pre-Roman* (*Early Iron Age*) *bronze shield from the Thames at Battersea*

pre-Roman British art, and some experts would attribute it to a somewhat later period than Caesar's invasion. In any case it is only one of a considerable number of weapons, dagger-sheaths, shield-ornaments and the like, of various dates in the Early Iron Age, found in the river-bed between Chelsea and Richmond, and now to be seen in the British and London Museums. Fewer are recorded from lower down the river, but a notable find in this category is the splendid horned helmet of bronze, probably of the first century BC, found in the Thames at Waterloo Bridge and now in the British Museum. (*Fig. 4.*) Like the Battersea shield this should probably be regarded as an object for parade rather than battle.

This brings us to a vexed question: how was all this valuable equipment lost? A single great battle can certainly be ruled out, in view of the wide range in date of these finds. We have concentrated on the Early Iron Age, but Bronze Age weapons are even more numerous in this stretch of river; a fine Roman sword with decorated scabbard from Fulham, now in the British Museum, is probably of the first century AD; Anglo-Saxon and Viking spears, battle-axes and swords also occur between Battersea and Brentford. There are three possibilities, each of which may account for some of the losses. Some may in fact have been lost in battle, in skirmishes that took

17

place at various periods in this stretch of the Thames; some may have been accidentally dropped while crossing the river; others may have been deliberately thrown into the water as offerings to the gods —for votive deposits of weapons and other valuables in swamps, pools and streams were commonly made by the Celtic peoples of the Early Iron Age,[1] a practice that no doubt goes back to much earlier times and probably continued at least into the Roman period. It is clear that the first two kinds of loss, at least, and possibly all three, are most likely to occur in parts of the river that are frequently crossed. Heavy objects such as weapons would have sunk directly to the bottom, where they would quickly have become embedded in the mud. They are therefore unlikely to have been carried by the stream far from the place where they were dropped. The quantity of such finds in the river-bed between Kew and Battersea strongly suggests that there was more than one crossing-place below Brentford. Bridges over such a wide river are likely to have been beyond the engineering capabilities of the pre-Roman Britons, and their construction and upkeep would have demanded a political cohesion between the two sides of the river, which did not then exist. Crossings by boat were, of course, equally possible in nearly all parts of the Thames, and would not account for concentrations of finds in this particular area, unless we imagine that here, for many generations, there was some kind of ferry-service—which again seems highly improbable in a tribal society that tended to be politically divided by the river. It is more likely that the Thames could be crossed on foot in this part by means of fords—and not only in one place.

The river today is very different from what it was in pre-Roman and Roman times, for the change in water-level has carried the tidal limit from below the present London Bridge upstream to Teddington. At Brentford[2] Romano-British wattle hut-floors have been found on the foreshore at or below the present level of low tide. (*Fig. 5.*) From this and other similar observations of Roman occupation levels at Tilbury and Southwark, it can be estimated that the river in early Roman times was more than twelve feet lower than the point it now reaches in an average high spring tide, and it may easily have been as much as fourteen feet lower in the first century BC. This part of the Thames is not very deep at low tide, when the water is nearer its level of two thousand years ago.

[1] T. G. E. Powell: *The Celts*, pp. 147–51.
[2] *Antiquity*, III, p. 20.

Fig. 5 Romano-British wattle hut floor excavated at low tide in the foreshore at Brentford

It is therefore hard to believe that the crossing at Brentford was half as difficult as the one described by Caesar, or that if he had gone so far upstream he could have thought that there was only one place where the river could be forded. It would be more consistent with his characteristic directness of action if, knowing that the territory of his principal antagonist lay beyond the Thames, he had made his way to a nearer point in the river, and had then followed it until he reached the first possible crossing-place. This was clearly a regular, though difficult, ford in territory controlled by Cassivellaunus, since it was fortified against him. It is significant, however, that while he was trying to penetrate into the interior after crossing, he was contacted by envoys of the Trinovantes, whose territory certainly did not extend west of the Lea valley. This tribe subsequently supplied him with the corn that he needed. These circumstances suggest that Caesar was operating not far from the eastern limits of Catuvellaunian territory, as would have been the case if he had crossed the Thames in what is now central London, rather than farther west. Whether this was at Chelsea, Westminster, or even farther downstream can only be surmised.

By the time of the invasion of Claudius, almost a century later, the political centre of gravity in Britain had moved to the east, as a result of the continued expansion of the Catuvellauni at the expense of the Trinovantes. Verulamium (St Albans) was abandoned as a royal seat by Cunobelinus, probably the great-grandson of Cassivellaunus, in favour of Camulodunum (Colchester), tribal centre of the conquered Trinovantes. This was of course much more convenient for trade with the Continent, which had become increasingly important, and was a source of wealth and luxury for the Belgic kings.

Unlike Julius Caesar, the invaders of AD 43 had come to stay, and had a definite plan of conquest, in which the fall of Camulodunum was to be the climax of the initial phase. This was to be achieved by the Emperor himself, partly to gain the confidence of his subjects, to whom he seemed a remarkably unimpressive figure, and partly to satisfy his own sense of historical purpose. Since Claudius was no soldier, there is little doubt that his victory was to be made as easy as possible. Like the great Julius, he was to cross the Thames and seize the capital of Britain's most powerful kingdom, but neither he nor his military advisers can have intended that he should encounter any serious opposition. He did not therefore accompany the army in its initial invasion, which was led by Aulus Plautius, an experienced general who was destined to be the first governor of Britain. The main force landed at Richborough, where the fortifications of its first base can still be seen, and after winning the decisive (though by no means easy) victory of the campaign at the Medway crossing, pursued the retreating Britons to the Thames.

Unfortunately the only surviving account of the next events was written more than 150 years later, and is probably not accurate in points of detail. According to this, the Britons retreated to the Thames, 'near where it empties into the ocean and at flood-tide forms a lake'. They knew the easy crossing-places and had no difficulty in getting to the north side of the river, but the pursuing auxiliary cavalry was less successful. Some swam across and others 'got over by a bridge a little way upstream'. They were able to cut off and destroy many of the Britons, but in trying to pursue the remainder lost a number of men in the swamps.[1]

[1] Cassius Dio: *History*, Loeb translation, VII, 419.

Fig. 6 *Roman officer's sword, with decoration on sheath representing Romulus and Remus, 1st century* AD, *from the Thames at Fulham*

Evidently the lower crossing-place was in the tidal part of the Thames, just below the site later occupied by Londinium, and even here the account suggests that the river was partly fordable at low tide by those who were familiar with it. The German auxiliaries were not, or were caught by the tide and had to swim. Some of the Roman troops may have crossed by the regular fords much farther upstream, for a sword that may well have been carried by one of the invaders was found in the river at Fulham. (*Fig. 6.*)

The reference to a bridge is intriguing, since, although it is not impossible that a pre-conquest bridge may have existed somewhere in this part of the Thames, it seems most unlikely, for the reasons already discussed, and in any case it is hardly credible that the Britons would have left it intact for the use of their enemies. Moreover, the bridge is described as being only a little way upstream from the tidal part of the river—i.e. not far from the City area, where a pre-conquest bridge would have had no purpose. The most likely explanation is that Dio telescoped two events—the initial crossing in hot pursuit of the Britons, and a subsequent crossing of the main force by means of a temporary bridge, which the Romans made themselves. A light structure of rafts could have been assembled very quickly if, as might be expected, their engineers had come prepared for the task.

c

If the first bridging of the Thames took place in the Southwark/ City area, the Roman officers who selected the spot either showed outstanding judgment, or—more probably—were well briefed in advance. The Thames and south-eastern Britain were now well-known to foreign traders, to say nothing of the British refugees who had thrown in their lot with the Romans. It seems likely therefore that the invaders would have been supplied with adequate topographical information before they left Gaul. Alternatively we may suppose that the first temporary bridge was built elsewhere, though evidently not far away, and that a careful reconnaissance then showed the best possible place for a permanent bridge and supply-base.

The construction of both is likely to have followed almost immediately—probably before the arrival of the Emperor to capture Camulodunum, for we can surely discount Dio's statement that he fought a battle to cross the Thames, in view of Claudius' own claim in the inscription in his triumphal arch, confirmed by Suetonius, that he suffered no losses in Britain. When the army of Aulus Plautius arrived in the neighbourhood of London, about the beginning of July AD 43, Claudius was still in Italy, possibly through a miscalculation of the amount of resistance likely to be encountered in the first phase of the campaign. It would have taken altogether about six weeks for the news of the Medway victory and Plautius' 'appeal for help' to reach him, and then for him to travel from Ostia to Britain. In the meantime, we cannot imagine that Aulus Plautius would have allowed his main force to kick their heels in idleness on the banks of the Thames, leaving only his left wing, the Second Legion under the future Emperor Vespasian, to continue an active campaign in the south and south-west. According to the pre-arranged plan he could not attack Camulodunum, which was obviously the next step, but he could keep his men busy with the considerable task of building a permanent bridge across the Thames, and constructing a base as a springboard for future conquests north of the river. Julius Caesar had built a pile bridge across the Rhine in ten days after the collection of timber had begun,[1] so it would have been quite possible for Claudius to have found a substantial bridge already complete when he arrived with his praetorian guards and corps of elephants.

Since the origin of London was the direct result of a military decision, probably taken in AD 43, we must consider the situation

[1] Julius Caesar: *The Conquest of Gaul*, (trans. S. A. Handford), Penguin Classics, 1951, pp. 116 f.

as it appeared to the general staff of Aulus Plautius, and try to determine the reasons for this choice.

It was clear that the Thames was a barrier bisecting the part of Britain that was most important to the Romans—the more developed and populous corn-producing region of the lowland zone. To unify it and bring both sections under firm control, it was necessary that the river should be permanently bridged. This was a first priority, as the centre of British political power, which the Emperor was determined to make the capital of the new province, lay in the northern section, and the ports that were most accessible from Gaul were in the southern. To provide the shortest overland link between the Channel ports and Camulodunum, it was necessary to build the bridge as near the river-mouth as possible. The lower part of the river, however, was subject to the rise and fall of the tides, a phenomenon regarded with considerable respect by the Romans, whose technique of bridge-building had been developed in the tideless rivers of the Mediterranean. Moreover, the estuary was broad, and the river unembanked, so that at high tide the lower part of the Thames, as Dio tells us, was like a lake. It was therefore necessary to find a place above the tidal limit, but only just above it, where the ground on both sides provided a firm and well-drained approach. The areas of alluvial silt were not very suitable, even where the surface was high enough to be safe from flooding, as piles would have been necessary to support the approach to the waterside as well as the bridge itself. On the north side there were several places just above the tidal limit where the lowest gravel terrace came near the water's edge, and would have provided an excellent approach for a bridge—in the neighbourhoods of Limehouse, the City and the Strand. South of the river in this area, however, the gravel was set farther back, and the river was bordered by alluvial silt. At Lambeth, the only place where the southern gravels reached the river, there was an extensive area of silt on the opposite side in Westminster. In Southwark and Bermondsey the border of silt was relatively narrow, and at one place it was interrupted by a spit of sand a few feet higher than the ground on either side. The Roman, with a soldier's eye for country, observed this small area of dry and open heath that extended to the river, contrasting with the lusher vegetation of the more low-lying land to the east and west, perhaps not yet a marsh, as it was soon to become, but ill-drained and intersected by creeks. He saw, too, that on the opposite side of the river was a low hill or plateau,

23

rising immediately from the waterside and only lightly wooded, with many open spaces.

At this point, then, both sides of the Thames offered a firm, dry bank for a bridgehead above the disturbing fluctuations of the tides. One other consideration must have been present in the military mind that made the decision: a bridge was vulnerable and Britain was not yet conquered. Was the position defensible? Here again the site had definite advantages. On the southern bank, the eastern flank was protected by a water-channel, observed in 1958 when New Guy's House was built. This stream was shallow, but was about twenty-five feet wide, and with its marshy valley would have presented a considerable obstacle.[1] Its mouth may have been between Hays Lane and Battle Bridge Lane, where there is still an inlet. It is possible that there was a similar channel on the western side, in the neighbourhood of Park Street, but this remains to be proved.[2] On the northern bank, the mouth and valley of a tributary stream could be seen just to the west of the position now occupied by Cannon Street Railway Station, and it was clear that this would give some protection to the northern bridgehead.

The decision was made, and the bridge was begun from the sandy heath now buried 13 feet below the northern part of Borough High Street. The choice was to determine the focal point of Britain's communications throughout the Roman occupation and through all subsequent ages until the present day, and was to create one of the greatest cities in the world. The first London Bridge, built by the legionaries of Aulus Plautius from the timber of the virgin woodlands near by, probably did not last as long as Roman rule in Britain, but the topographical pattern was set, and in spite of changing conditions in the river itself, which swept the tidal waters farther upstream, the succeeding bridges in wood and stone have never been moved very far from the original position. We do not know exactly where this was, but almost certainly it lay a little way downstream from the present bridge. The last wooden bridge stood in late Anglo-Saxon and Norman times nearly 90 yards downstream from the modern bridge, with its northern end at the bottom of Pudding Lane.[3] When the foundations of London Bridge became unsafe, its successor could never be built on exactly the same site,

[1] *LAMAS Trans.*, XXI pt. 2 (1965), pp. 123–8.
[2] M. R. Maitland Muller: 'Southwark—Roman Suburb', *Guy's Hospital Gazette*, 26 December 1964, pp. 5–6.
[3] Miss M. B. Honeybourne: 'Norman London', *London and Middlesex Historian*, no. 3, October 1966, p. 11.

since, apart from the great technical difficulty of replacing the decayed piles with sound ones, it was necessary to keep the old bridge in daily use until the new one was complete. As in the last thousand years the position has been moved a little way upstream with each rebuilding, it might be expected that the Roman wooden bridge, which cannot possibly have survived for a thousand years, was a short distance downstream from its Anglo-Saxon successor. A possible position for a Roman bridge—not necessarily the first—is about 150 yards downstream from the present London Bridge. In 1834, when excavations for a sewer were made in Lower Thames Street near the ancient water-front, it was found that there was a concentration of wooden piles, larger than those found elsewhere, at the bottom of Botolph Lane,[1] which, as we shall see, seems to be on the line of a Roman street leading to Bishopsgate and the road to the north. This street was not laid out until more than a quarter of a century after the conquest, however, so cannot be part of an original road to the north from the bridgehead.[2] The piles observed could, of course, be of any date, and are as likely to have supported a wharf or pier as a bridgehead. This is probably the most easterly position that is possible for a bridge within the limits of the Southwark sand-spit.

There is, however, some evidence to suggest that there was a Roman bridge on or near the site of Old London Bridge, the first stone bridge, begun in 1176, which stood about 35 yards downstream from the present bridge. When it was demolished in 1831, extensive dredging operations took place where it had stood, in order to deepen the channel. In the course of this work, quantities of Roman antiquities, including coins of all dates, were brought up from the bed of the river. Their presence suggests rather strongly that the regular crossing-place was here, and Roach Smith, the great London antiquary who collected them, was firmly convinced that many of the coins had been deliberately deposited in the river as votive offerings on occasions when the bridge was repaired.[3] Moreover the line of Stane Street in Southwark, though not yet determined with absolute certainty, seems to be pointing to a position very near Old London Bridge.[4] This is also consistent with the street-plan of the Roman city, the lay-out of which is likely to

[1] R. Kelsey: *A Description of the Sewers of the City of London* (MS book, in the charge of the City Engineer), p. 90.
[2] *RCL*, pp. 117–18.
[3] *IRL*, pp. 20–1; also *Arch.*, XXIX (1842), pp. 161–6.
[4] K. M. Kenyon: *Excavations in Southwark*, p. 12. But see also pp. 57–8 of the present book.

have been influenced by the position of the bridgehead. A modern (and medieval) street, Fish Street Hill, leads straight from the site of Old London Bridge practically to the central axis of the basilica/ forum block, and to a position occupied by two earlier buildings of importance. (*See p. 100.*) It would not be surprising if a Roman street, leading from the bridge to the heart of the city, lay almost on this same line.

Nevertheless, although there are several scraps of evidence pointing generally in the direction of the medieval bridge for the site of its Roman predecessor, they prove to be contradictory if one attempts to determine its precise position. Old London Bridge with its starlings occupied a considerable area, and it is not clear where the Roman antiquities were mostly found. Syer Cuming mentions wooden piles and Roman coins just *east* of the stone bridge,[1] whereas Roach Smith specifically states that a concentration of the coins was found about twelve yards from the second arch of the *new* bridge, a position well to the west of it.

Excavations in 1967, on the southern approach to Old London Bridge in Tooley Street, were inconclusive, largely because there was a great deal of later disturbance, and very little of the early levels survived. A layer of gravel metalling a few inches thick, overlying natural silt, was found in a very limited area immediately opposite the eastern half of the medieval bridge. To the west of this were traces of a Roman building and Roman pits, while to the east of it was marshy ground, which seems to have been unoccupied in early Roman times. The gravel layer was pierced by three large holes, which had evidently contained the pile foundations of a very substantial wooden structure. It was clear that this was the only possible position for a Roman bridge within the small area investigated where early levels survived, and it seemed possible that the gravel surface was a hard, giving access to an early pontoon bridge, and that the post-holes were the foundations of a later pile bridge. No trace of the Roman road leading to the bridge was found, but this would presumably have terminated farther south, as the pile bridge would have crossed the river at a considerable height, and would therefore have required a long approach. No dating evidence for the piles was found until the very end of the excavation, when a bronze coin, evidently votive, was found under a piece of Roman tile at the bottom of one of the post-holes. The coin was unde-

[1] *JBAA*, 1st Ser., XLIII (1887), pp. 162-3.

cipherable, but was presumably of late date, probably fourth-century, as it was only half an inch in diameter.[1] It is inconceivable that no pile bridge was built before late Roman times, so we are left with two possible explanations. The first, favoured by the excavator, is that the pile structure was a pier or jetty, in which case we must look elsewhere for the bridge—presumably upstream, beyond the limits that could be investigated, since a large jetty for shipping is likely to be downstream of the bridge. The second is that this was in fact the position of the bridge, and that the votive coin was deposited—in striking confirmation of Roach Smith's view—when this portion of it was rebuilt in late Roman times. Here the problem must be left until more evidence emerges.

It is inconceivable that the northern bridgehead was left unfortified, although no early military defences have yet been identified. Since they would be represented only by filled-in ditches and the remains of earth embankments, however, they are unlikely to be detected in a builders' excavation, and there have been few opportunities for scientific archaeological investigation in the eastern part of the City. Since the western flank was protected by the Walbrook, the more important defensive lines were presumably placed to the north and east of Cornhill. When these were laid out, London was born.

[1] I am very much indebted to Mr G. Beeby for the main facts of this excavation, generously given in advance of his own report. The interpretation, however, is mine, and is based on the information available to me at the time of writing. It does not necessarily foreshadow Mr Beeby's final views.

CHAPTER TWO

Roman London as a Centre of Communications

THE BIRTH OF LONDON

The bridgehead on the north side of the Thames was an obvious place for a military base, and its use for this purpose is likely to have followed immediately after the building of the bridge. If the suggestion is correct that the first London Bridge was built in the early months of the conquest, it must be assumed that the establishment of a London base was likewise very early, and it is even possible that Claudius rode out from it to conquer Camulodunum. In default of definite evidence, however, any attempt to reconstruct the beginning of London can only be conjecture based on geographical and historical probabilities, within the framework of the very few known facts. The sequence of events—the birth of a military base from a fortified bridgehead—is likely to be correct, but it could have occurred either at the very beginning of the conquest or a little later.

After the fall of Camulodunum, the Roman army was divided into two main parts. In the south and west, the Second Legion, commanded by the future Emperor Vespasian—probably with some assistance from their British allies, the Regni of West Sussex—was engaged in mopping-up pockets of resistance and in pushing on into the south-west. Meanwhile the other three legions were operating to the north of the Thames, fanning out into the north, central and western Midlands. One of their main bases is likely to have been near Camulodunum, where early military tombstones have been found, but its precise position has never been identified archaeologically.

In recent years scholars have tended to disregard London in connexion with this phase of the conquest, yet its part must have been at least as great as that of the hypothetical base in Essex. Some link in communications between the troops campaigning in the south-west and those in the Midlands was essential, and if a Thames-side base did not already exist, it must now have been necessary to create it. Political considerations may have demanded that the principal headquarters of the Governor should be at or near Camulodunum, but London would have been a much more convenient nerve centre for the direction of the whole campaign, and it is difficult to believe that its advantages would have been ignored for very long. Be this as it may, there is no doubt that it soon became the main base for supplies arriving from the Continent, since the possibility of direct access by ships would quickly have been realized. The North Foreland presented some hazards, but the long haul overland from the Channel ports was avoided. For many purposes, no doubt, including the transport of troops from the south, the shorter sea passage continued to be preferred, but ships crossing from the mouth of the Rhine, where Claudius had recently established forts such as Valkenburg for communication with Britain, could most conveniently sail directly for the Thames, and could reach the point where it was bridged. They could also, of course, go straight to the Essex estuaries near Camulodunum, but although supplies undoubtedly reached the Roman armies by this route, no port of any significance seems to have developed there, so that the superiority of the Thames as a gateway to Britain was clearly recognized from the beginning.

There is abundant evidence for occupation in London during the reign of Claudius, in the form of closely datable imported pottery of the mid-first century and earlier, mostly, though not exclusively, found to the east of the Walbrook and on the south bank of the Thames near London Bridge.[1] A very similar distribution has been found for coins of Claudius and earlier reigns.[2] There is good reason, therefore, to believe that the first London was in the eastern angle made by the Walbrook and the Thames, with some occupation of the southern bridgehead also. Unfortunately, we know practically nothing of its lay-out or structures. Post-holes indicating the presence of huts, apparently of very early date, were observed in 1955–6 during the builders' excavations on the site of the Chase National Bank of New York, Plough Court, on the south

[1] *Arch.*, LXXVIII, pp. 73–110.
[2] Ibid., LXVI, p. 271, fig. 25; *London in R. Times*, pp. 190–1.

side of Lombard Street,[1] and near by, on the site of Barclays Bank on the north side of the same street, was found a large trench, which had been filled in during the Claudian period.[2] This was U-shaped in section, and its purpose is unknown: it was neither a defensive ditch nor a drain, and may possibly have served as a latrine. It certainly belongs to a very early phase in the occupation of London, probably before the first streets were laid out. This was not long delayed, however, and an east–west gravelled street was constructed in this area in the first years of the Roman occupation.[3] Part of it underlies the eastern end of Lombard Street, where there seems to have been a city street throughout London's history.

Although a considerable amount of Roman military equipment has been found in the City of London, especially in or near the stream-bed of the Walbrook,[4] it cannot for the most part be closely dated. We know that there was a Roman garrison in London in the second century, and this may have been responsible for many of the losses. There is no direct evidence, therefore, either from structures or small finds, that the first occupation of London was military, and that its first function was as a supply-base for the armies of Aulus Plautius and his successor Ostorius Scapula. This can be deduced, however, from the fact that a town had developed here within a few years of the invasion and was soon linked with the newly conquered territory to the north-east, north, north-west, west and south, and also with the Channel ports, by an admirable series of trunk roads, which, with minor deviations, are still in use today. The connecting link between these roads was the bridge over the Thames and the settlement that seems to have been already laid out at the northern bridgehead. If it had not been, the roads on the north side of the river would presumably have met at the bridge itself, and would almost certainly have left their mark on the subsequent topo-graphy of the city in the form of a radiating street-plan—for which we have no evidence at all.

The predominance of London in the Roman road-system is demonstrated by the fact that the Antonine Itinerary, a road-book probably of the early third century, begins or ends seven of its fifteen routes in Britain at Londinium, which is also an inter-mediate station on an eighth. Thanks to the roadways cut through

[1] *RCL*, 289.
[2] *RCL*, 243; *LAMAS Trans.*, XXI, pt. 1 (1963) p. 72.
[3] *RCL*, 290.
[4] Listed by Dr Graham Webster in *Arch. Journ.*, CXV (1960), pp. 84–7. The objects are mostly in the British, London and Guildhall Museums.

the surrounding woodlands at an early date in the Roman period, London was already what it has remained ever since—a great distributing centre, where land- and water-routes met. It is not surprising that within seventeen years of the Roman invasion London had become the flourishing emporium of private enterprise. But the great Roman roads were not laid out for the benefit of the traders: their primary purpose was the subjugation and pacification of the new province. They were made by soldiers for the rapid movement of troops and equipment, and for the maintenance of communications between the various parts of the army. The convergence of these roads on London is in itself convincing evidence that a military supply-base was situated there at the time of their construction. Many of the towns of Roman Britain that were not built on the sites of earlier tribal centres owed their origin to the presence of army bases. There seems little doubt that London should be numbered among them.

Although the major Roman roads that converged on Londinium were almost certainly of military origin and of early date, in due course the city's trade and the need of its population for the produce of the countryside demanded also a network of minor roads. Military engineers may have played their part in the construction of these, but their primary purpose was for daily convenience rather than military strategy. Whereas the great roads have survived, with considerable modification, as modern highways, the lesser roads usually remain in the open country only as broken alignments of lanes, sometimes linked by boundaries, and in the built-up area are in most cases quite unrecognizable, although they may survive in part as modern streets that are the descendants of country lanes.

A Roman road in the London area was made of the local gravel, closely rammed to produce a hard surface, slightly above the surrounding ground where this was level and well drained, and built up as a considerably raised causeway when passing through water-logged hollows. On soft and unstable ground it was sometimes supported by timber piles, and retaining walls of ragstone, gravel concrete or even timber were very occasionally used.[1] In a few instances the gravel was covered with a metalling of flint nodules, ragstone and other material,[2] but the date of this is suspect, and usually in London gravel alone was used. The road-surface was

[1] See *RCHM : RL*, p. 64; *RCL*, 251 & 296.
[2] *RCHM :RL*, p. 54; *Ant. Journ.*, IV, p. 409 & V, p. 166.

cambered for drainage into shallow ditches or gullies, which bordered the road on both sides. When it needed repair a new layer of gravel was put on top and was likewise closely rammed to make a new surface. As the years passed, if the road continued to be maintained, a considerable thickness of characteristically hard gravel metalling was built up. It is often described as gravel concrete, but it is unlikely that mortar was always added to the gravel. The cementing seems often to have been due to the infiltration of mud among the closely packed pebbles, but the result was an intensely hard and surprisingly smooth surface.

The ancient roads surviving as modern highways, occasionally as minor streets, and more rarely as vestigial remains on open land, are almost the only visible traces left by the Romans in London outside the City. Moreover, this is a field of archaeological investigation where many problems remain to be solved, and in which the amateur who is aware of the present state of our knowledge may easily make an important contribution in his own suburb. Even without digging himself, by careful observation of local excavations carried out for a variety of non-archaeological purposes, he may be able to confirm, correct or disprove a current theory. This will only be possible, however, if he knows where to look and what he is likely to see. The supposed courses of the Roman roads through Greater London, reasonably certain in some cases and very doubtful in others, will therefore be considered in detail in the next two chapters, together with some account of the investigations that have already taken place.

ROMAN LONDON AS A PORT

Before discussing the individual roads, however, we must first turn to another route, which contributed more than any of these to the establishment of London as the principal centre of communications in Britain. This was the great water-highway from the open sea to the interior, provided by the River Thames, which had been exploited by invaders and traders for centuries. The bridgehead settlement with its network of landward communications now became the natural terminus of water-borne traffic, although the remains of two large sailing-ships of Roman date upstream of the bridge testify that the latter was not an impassable barrier. It must be assumed that it had a drawbridge section that could be raised to allow the passage of masted vessels, like Tower Bridge today.

In Roman times, as now, the river-traffic was of two kinds. Sea-going ships brought cargoes of fine pottery, wine, olive-oil and manufactured luxury goods of many kinds from the Continent, and carried out British exports of cloth, hides, furs and lead. River-barges carried heavy freight such as building-stone, which it was difficult to transport by land, from one part of the Thames and its tributaries to another.

The position of the docks of Londinium is unknown, and wharf-like timber structures recorded in the lower part of King William Street (on the site of Regis House, for example) seem to be too far inland. They are more likely to have been used for terracing the hillside where the river-bank rose steeply, like the chalk platforms on wooden piles seen at Lambeth Hill.[1] It is probable that the docks extended along the river-front, below and above the bridge, beneath the line of Thames Street, where massive walls, formerly believed to be part of the defensive city wall, have come to light from time to time.[2] Some of these may well have been quays. It used to be thought that the stream of the Walbrook served as a dock, but this seems quite impossible, as its channel was only 12–14 feet wide. Small lighters may have been able to enter it, one at a time, at least in the earlier period when the banks were revetted, but such traffic must have been of very limited importance. It is true that dockers' tools, such as the hooks used for handling sacks and bales, a case-opener, baling-needle and crane-hook, have been found in the bed of the stream, but so have the tools of many other trades, including those of stone-masons, plasterers and even surgeons, who are unlikely to have worked there. The abundance of such objects may be accounted for by the presence on the banks of the Walbrook of a great emporium where hardware of this kind was sold; or possibly by some superstitious practice, in which the tools of one's trade were on occasion devoted to the gods by dropping them into the stream. (*See pp. 176–7.*)

The remains of three ships of the Roman period have been found in London, and, with the exception of two Scandinavian rowing-vessels, they are the only ships of this date to have been discovered, so far, outside the Mediterranean area. The first of these was found in 1910 on the site of County Hall, Lambeth, and a portion of it, very much reconstructed, is at present preserved in the store-rooms of the London Museum at Lancaster House. This

[1] *RCL*, 304, 306, 308, 110.
[2] Ibid., 114, 123, 261, 354.

consists of a large piece of the bottom and one side from the central part of the vessel, 38 feet in length, and built of oak. It has been estimated that the complete ship was 60–70 feet long and 15–16 feet wide. It is carvel-built (i.e. the planks are edge to edge), and the shell of planking was constructed before the ribs were inserted. In these respects, and in the way in which the bottom planks were jointed to the keel and to each other, the vessel resembles the Roman ships found in the Mediterranean, although the species of oak used shows that it was built in northern Europe. The lack of any arrangement for rowing, and the presence of a pulley-block and possible belaying-pin indicate that it was probably a sailing-ship. Coins of Tetricus I, Carausius and Allectus, found beneath ribs and on the bottom of the vessel, show that it sank after AD 293, but probably not very long after. The possibility that it was sunk during the disturbances in the London area following the defeat of Allectus in 296 cannot be entirely ruled out, especially as a large stone is said to have been found embedded in one of the strakes, in a way that suggested it had arrived with considerable force. It is quite clear, however, that the vessel, with its rounded and un-strengthened hull, was not a warship, and its sinking in quiet waters at the edge of the river, so far upstream from the port, may have been simply the means of disposing of a superannuated and un-serviceable craft. It was at one time thought to be a river-barge, but the subsequent discovery of true barges of Roman date has shown that it is of quite a different character. Although considerably smaller than the Mediterranean merchant vessels (about 60 tons, compared with their tonnage of 70–340 or more) it is of essentially similar type, and is most likely to have been a small cargo-ship.[1]

The other two vessels were probably river-barges, with the flat bottoms suitable for carrying bulk cargo in shallow waters. The first was found by Peter Marsden in 1958, on the site of New Guy's House, a new surgical block of Guy's Hospital, Bermondsey. It was first uncovered in a foundation trench at the south-west corner of the building, and a small archaeological excavation was subsequently carried out on adjoining ground. The vessel lay in a creek or tributary of the Thames, where it had apparently been abandoned. The north end—it is uncertain whether it was the bow or the stern—pointed in a north-north-easterly direction, and the ship was traced for a length of 22 feet. It has been estimated that its total

[1] P. R. V. Marsden: 'The County Hall Ship', *LAMAS Trans.*, XXI, pt. 2 (1965), pp. 109–17; *London in R. Times*, pp. 151–4.

length was probably about 50 feet, and its breadth about 14 feet. Like the County Hall ship, it was carvel-built, and was constructed of oak of the northern species. In other respects, however, it was of a totally different construction. There was no evidence that the planks had ever been jointed, and they were attached to the ribs by clenched iron nails. The framework of ribs must therefore have been constructed first, a method of shipbuilding generally used in more recent times in north-western Europe, but not practised in the Roman period on the Mediterranean. A caulking of crushed hazel-twigs was found in one of the seams. The vessel lay at a depth of about 16 feet below the present surface, and was covered by stratified silt deposits containing only Roman pottery. These in turn were sealed by layers of silt, more than $3\frac{1}{2}$ feet thick, which contained no pottery at all. The dating evidence suggests that the boat was abandoned about AD 200.[1]

The third ship was also found by Peter Marsden. Fragments of an ancient wreck were brought to light by an excavation in the bed of the Thames in September, 1962, during work on the Blackfriars Bridgehead Improvement Scheme. It lay between the road-bridge and the railway-bridge about 20 yards south of the old embankment, and at first could only be investigated with great difficulty at low spring tides. Fortunately, in the following summer a coffer-dam for the construction of the new embankment wall was built across the southern portion of the wreck, and within this oblong box it was possible to carry out an archaeological excavation, and subsequently to remove for detailed study the timbers that were enclosed. (*Fig. 7*.) The remainder of the ship still lies buried in the mud beneath the new embankment. The attempted conservation of the pieces that were removed was carried out under difficult conditions in the Royal Exchange, with inadequate facilities. It was unsuccessful, and the wood is now badly split, but the timbers have been preserved, and could, of course, be restored in plaster like those of the County Hall vessel. It is doubtful, however, whether it will be possible to assemble this portion of an ancient ship for public exhibition.

The Blackfriars ship was carvel-built, without joints between the planks, which were attached to the ribs by enormous iron nails. As with the Guy's House vessel, a framework of ribs had first been assembled, following a tradition of shipbuilding quite different from

[1] P. R. V. Marsden: 'A Boat of the Roman Period discovered on the Site of New Guy's House, Bermondsey, 1958', *LAMAS Trans.*, XXI, pt. 2 (1965), pp. 118–31.

Fig. 7 *Roman ship, as excavated in coffer-dam at Blackfriars, 1962*

that of the classical world. There was no keel, but the ship had a
stem-post and stern-post; the bottom was flat, and there was a well-
marked angle or chine where it rose to meet the side. A similar
feature is found in modern Thames barges, the purpose being to
broaden the base so that the vessel will sit upright when resting on
the river-bed at low tide. The proportions of the Blackfriars ship
were also barge-like, with a breadth of about 22 feet to a length of
50–55 feet. Its function was finally demonstrated conclusively by
the discovery of the forward edge of the cargo, which consisted of
large lumps of Kentish ragstone, quarried in the Maidstone district
of Kent and much used in Roman London for building material.
There seems no doubt that the vessel was a river-barge engaged in
the transport of the stone down the Medway and up the Thames,
where it finally met disaster at the mouth of the Fleet. This seems
to have been due to an accident, as the cargo had apparently shifted
to the port side, and there was some indication that the stern
portion had been severed from the rest of the ship. The starboard
side had collapsed inwards a considerable time after the ship had
sunk, and overlay gravel that had been washed into the wreck
while it lay on the river-bottom. This layer contained pottery
fragments of the first, second and third centuries, with nothing that
need be later than the second half of the third century. It seems
likely, therefore, that the ship finally broke up on the river-bed
during the latter part of the third century, but the wreck probably
occurred considerably earlier. A number of Roman objects, which
were either on board when the ship sank or were washed in
immediately afterwards, were found in a layer of silt on the bottom
of the vessel. They included fragments of a bowl of the late first
or early second century; a wooden mallet, possibly used for caulking; and a leather panel, perhaps from a pouch or wallet, with a
perforated decoration in the form of a dolphin. In view of its
nautical device, it seems quite likely that the last object was in use
aboard the barge, and, if it was a pouch, it may even have contained the ship's papers. More puzzling was an unfinished millstone
made of stone from the Pennines—a curious find in a Thames barge
carrying ragstone from Kent. An important piece of dating evidence

37

was found in a rectangular socket that was cut into the seventh floor-timber, evidently to contain the base of a fixed mast or a mast-pillar supporting a tabernacle at deck-level for a hinged mast. No trace of mast or mast-pillar remained, and it had evidently either been washed away or salvaged. In the socket or mast-step, however, lay a copper coin (*as*) of the Emperor Domitian, struck in AD 88–9. It had evidently been put there for luck when the mast was fitted, in accordance with a custom that has survived to the present day. The coin was somewhat worn and must have been in circulation for a number of years before it was put in the mast-step, presumably when the barge was built. It was evidently selected for its reverse type, which appropriately shows Fortuna, goddess of good luck, holding a ship's rudder. The Blackfriars barge, therefore, was probably built in the first half of the second century; it was in service long enough for its timbers to become badly infested with maritime worms (*Teredo*), and was apparently wrecked between the late second and mid-third century.[1]

One very important fact has been established by Peter Marsden after research into these two ancient wrecks. The port of Londinium owed its origin to the Romans; many of the ships that used it did not. Those that were concerned purely with river-traffic, at least, seem to have been constructed according to a tradition that was alien to the shipbuilders of the Mediterranean—and equally alien to the seafaring barbarians of the north, who were already making the clinker-built, oar-propelled vessels that were to become the terror of a later age. Marsden has pointed out the remarkable similarities between the Blackfriars barge and the ships of the Veneti, a Celtic tribe of north-west Gaul, described by Julius Caesar. Both were sailing-vessels, not propelled by oars, with flat bottoms for use in shallow waters; both were very solidly built to withstand rough usage, with hulls made entirely of oak; and both had cross-timbers a foot wide, which were secured with huge iron nails 'as thick as a man's thumb'.[2] It is clear that the Thames barges of Roman times were built in a tradition that owed little or nothing to Mediterranean civilization, but presumably originated in north-western Europe among the Celtic peoples of the pre-Roman Iron Age.

[1] The evidence briefly summarized here is dealt with fully in Mr P. R. V. Marsden's report, *A Roman Ship from Blackfriars, London*, published by Guildhall Museum in 1967. This also gives a detailed account of the construction of the ship.

[2] Ibid., pp. 34–5. See also Julius Caesar: *De Bello Gallico*, III, 13; or *The Conquest of Gaul*, (trans. S. A. Handford), Penguin Classics, 1951, pp. 98–9.

We do not know whether these vessels were built at London, but it is by no means unlikely that a shipbuilding industry would have developed in the neighbourhood of a busy port. There is, in fact, rather surprisingly, one scrap of actual documentary evidence that a citizen of Roman London was involved in some way with ship-building. Wooden tablets with waxed surfaces were commonly used for commercial correspondence, the writing being incised with a *stilus*. The point sometimes went right through the wax and marked the wood beneath, so that very occasionally legible words and phrases remain on the pinewood tablets, a number of which have been found in London, mostly preserved in the silt of the Walbrook. One example from Lothbury, now in the London Museum, refers to the construction of a ship and the making of a rudder, but is unfortunately too illegible to be fully translated.[1]

The three Roman ships from London so far discovered were cargo-vessels, and there was no doubt a preponderance of such craft at the quays of Londinium. Imperial war-galleys were probably as rarely to be seen as ships of the Royal Navy in the Port of London today. Nevertheless, our only contemporary representation of Londinium shows such a vessel on the waters of the Thames. This is the reverse of the unique gold medallion that commemorates the arrival of Constantius Chlorus at London in AD 296, when Britain was regained after the defeat of the usurper Allectus. The scene—showing Constantius on horseback welcomed by a kneeling figure, representing Londinium, before a city gate—is purely symbolical, but the galley on the Thames represents what actually occurred. The portion of the invading force under the direct command of the junior Emperor, after being lost in a fog, eventually rounded the North Foreland and sailed directly to London—just in time to save the city from being sacked by fugitives from the defeated army of Allectus. The circumstances were then exceptional, but it is by no means unlikely that on many other occasions warships dropped anchor at Londinium. It is even possible that some were actually based on the Thames, especially in the later period when piracy was rampant. This may perhaps explain the discovery in London of a small bronze model of the prow of a ship, now in the British Museum. (*Fig. 8.*) It represents a galley of the imperial fleet called the *Ammilla* ('Contest'), with the typical ram of a fighting ship. The inscription on it, AMMILLA AVG FELIX, refers to the good

---

[1] *London in R. Times*, pp. 54–5, fig. 9, 3.

fortune of the ship, and the model is much more likely to have been a votive offering to ensure this, than a trophy of some victory, as has been suggested. It would presumably have been dedicated by the captain or crew at a temple or other sacred place in Londinium.

Fig. 8 *Bronze model of prow of Roman war-galley from London ; length 3 in.*

CHAPTER THREE

Roman Roads
North of the River

Let us now trace the course of the Roman roads from Londinium as they pass through the Greater London of today, where many survive as important thoroughfares, although the modern highways have in some places departed slightly from the lines of the ancient roads, and in the built-up area of London it is often impossible to determine the exact position of the latter. (*See fig. 9.*)

Since it has been impracticable to include large-scale maps showing the roads described over such a great area, reference should be made in this chapter and the next to detailed street-plans, such as those in Bartholomew's Reference Atlas of Greater London.

THE COLCHESTER ROAD

The road to Colchester (Camulodunum), the first capital of the Roman province, was initially of great importance, and must have been one of the earliest permanent highways to be constructed. Even so, it does not seem to have started at the bridgehead, but from the eastern end of the nucleus of Londinium, which had already been laid out.[1] It left the Roman city at Aldgate, where a gateway was accordingly placed when the city wall was built; thence it followed the line of Aldgate High Street and presumably of Whitechapel High Street. Sections of the ancient gravel road-metalling were seen in 1938 when excavations were made for the extension of Aldgate East Underground station. The lowest layers rested on natural clay at a depth of ten feet below the present road-surface.

[1] It now seems certain that the roadway found under Great Eastcheap (now the eastern end of Cannon Street) in 1831, was not part of this road, but an east–west road. See *RCL*, p. 116.

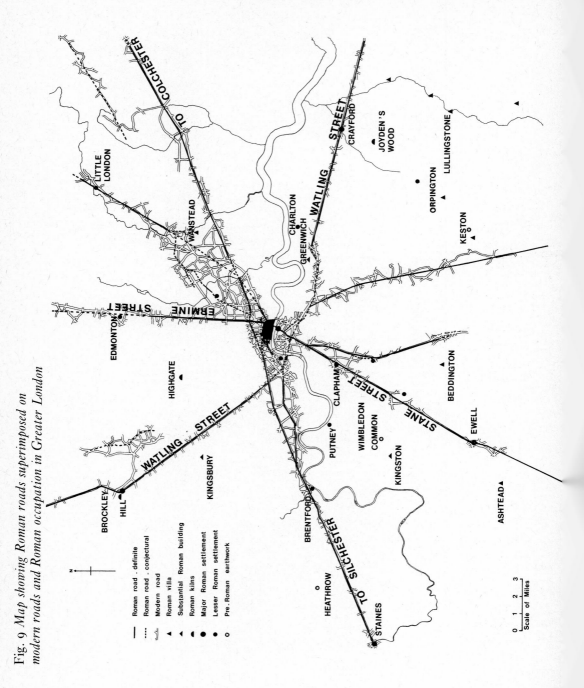

Fig. 9 *Map showing Roman roads superimposed on modern roads and Roman occupation in Greater London*

Roman road - definite
Roman road - conjectural
Modern road
Roman villa
Substantial Roman building
Roman kilns
Major Roman settlement
Lesser Roman settlement
Pre - Roman earthwork

N

TO COLCHESTER
LITTLE LONDON
WANSTEAD
ERMINE STREET
EDMONTON
HIGHGATE
WATLING STREET
BROCKLEY HILL
KINGSBURY
TO SILCHESTER
STAINES
HEATHROW
BRENTFORD
PUTNEY
CLAPHAM
WIMBLEDON COMMON
KINGSTON
STANE STREET
EWELL
ASHTEAD
BEDDINGTON
KESTON
WATLING STREET
CRAYFORD
JOYDEN'S WOOD
ORPINGTON
LULLINGSTONE
CHARLTON
GREENWICH

0 1 2 3
Scale of Miles

The course of the road eastward from Whitechapel High Street is quite unknown until it reached Old Ford, where it crossed the Lea. It clearly did not follow the modern Mile End Road and Bow Road, leading to Bow Bridge, which was not built until the twelfth century. The Roman ford was about half a mile farther upstream, in the neighbourhood of Iceland Wharf, where a large block of herring-bone-tile pavement, probably of Roman date, was found in the bed of the stream.[1] A number of Roman burials, both cremations of the first and second centuries and later inhumations have been found in the neighbourhood of Old Ford.[2]

Immediately to the east it is lost in the Stratford Marsh, until its line can be picked up in the modern Romford Road, where a complete section of an ancient gravel road was observed in front of the Passmore Edwards Museum in 1963. Under the modern road two gravel road-beds separated by a deposit of silt were found. Both had side-ditches for drainage, and both were intensely hard. The lower, with its surface four feet below the modern road-level, rested directly on the natural gravel and is believed to have been Roman.[3]

The modern road now seems to follow the Roman highway, perhaps with a minor deviation through Forest Gate and Manor Park, to the crossing of the River Roding at Ilford. It continues on the line of the ancient road through Ilford to Chadwell Heath, except for a slight deviation to the south where it crosses the railway line at Seven Kings Station. At Romford, however, it apparently departs a little from the Roman line, rejoining it on a more north-easterly alignment in the straight stretch of road between Gidea Park and Brentwood.

THE ROAD TO THE NORTH (ERMINE STREET)

The main road to Lincoln (Lindum) and the north was clearly accommodated by the gateway at Bishopsgate when the Roman city wall was built, but we do not know its original course farther south, or the way in which it was linked with the bridge. After the great remodelling of the central part of the city that took place in the half-century after about AD 80, it was linked with a north–south

---

[1] *Proc. Soc. Ant.*, XXIII (1909–11), pp. 236–7.

[2] *RCHM : RL*, p. 164.

[3] *The Essex Naturalist*, vol. 31, 3 (1964), pp. 208–12. The road may not have taken a direct course from Old Ford to this point, however, as a section of gravel metalling, which appeared to be the edge of a road, was seen by Mr Raymond Chaplin outside the Midland Bank in Stratford Broadway in 1965, a little to the south of the supposed line.

street that formed the eastern side of a square grid of streets framing the basilica and forum. This roadway is represented by gravel metalling observed in 1932 just to the east of Lime Street Passage.[1] Its line follows that of the modern streets of Philpot Lane and Botolph Lane to the river at a point which—as we have seen—is a possible position for the Roman bridge. (*See p. 25*.) This road, however, was not made before the Flavian period, since the gravel metalling overlay occupation debris of that date. It cannot therefore have been the original highway, although this may not have been far away.

If, as is more probable, the Roman bridge was on the site of Old London Bridge, a direct route from the bridgehead to Bishopsgate would have been on or near the line of Fish Street Hill and Gracechurch Street. We know, however, that important Roman public buildings straddled the northern half of Gracechurch Street from an early date, and it is most unlikely that an important thoroughfare would have been deliberately blocked by the Roman town-planners. It seems more probable that the road to the north did not begin at the bridgehead at all, but at the northern perimeter of a city nucleus that had already been laid out. This, like the apparent absence of any trace of a continuation of the Colchester road to the bridge, would suggest very strongly that Roman London began as a planned centre, rather than as a natural growth where important routes met.

It is clear that, after leaving the city by Bishopsgate, the course of the Roman road was identical with that of the modern street of Bishopsgate. Roman burials have been found on both sides of the street, and farther north, at 290 Bishopsgate, nearly five hundred yards beyond the city gate, two Roman ragstone walls with courses of bonding tiles were encountered during sewer-excavations in 1852. The western wall lay thirty feet behind the frontage of the east side of Bishopsgate, and the eastern twenty feet farther east.[2] Both were parallel with Bishopsgate—a significant fact if accurately recorded, since there is a slight change of direction in the modern street before this point is reached. As the Roman building is likely to have been aligned on the Roman highway, it suggests that the modern street of Bishopsgate follows the course of the latter very closely.

---

[1] *JRS*, XXIII (1933), p. 205; *RCL*, **232**.
[2] *RCHM: RL*, p. 145, where a note on a City Sewers plan is quoted.

Farther north the present highway continues along Shoreditch High Street, where there seems to be a slight departure from the ancient line, but after this the Roman road is probably followed exactly by Kingsland Road and High Street, Stoke Newington Road and High Street, Stamford Hill, High Road and Tottenham High Road. In Edmonton, however, the modern main road curves to the east along Fore Street, and it has been suggested that the Roman road continued straight on, taking the central prong of a three-way road fork along the line of a minor residential street called Snells Park.[1] A sewer-trench at the junction of this street and High Road in 1956 intersected 'a gravel bank about twenty feet wide bounded by side ditches', a description that might well be applied to an *agger*—the embankment of a Roman road. The observer, however, saw 'no trace of metalling', and was evidently convinced that it was not.[2] Farther north, a broad ridge along the edge of Pymmes Park was thought to be part of the *agger*, but this was investigated in 1956 and found to be a plain earth bank.[3] Margary suggested a continuation on the same alignment, crossing the Great Cambridge Road near Lincoln Road, and proceeding west of the arterial road to Forty Hill, north of which it is represented by the modern road, Bulls Cross. A series of excavations on this line in 1957, however, gave completely negative results,[4] and the precise course of Ermine Street through Edmonton and Enfield remains problematical, although its continuation to the north through Theobald's Park and Cheshunt seems to be well defined.

THE SILCHESTER ROAD

This was the great highway not only to Silchester (Calleva), the tribal capital of the Atrebates, but beyond it to all parts of south-western Britain. Within Londinium it was the westward continuation of the main east–west street, the *via principalis* of the early city, a portion of which still survives as a city street at the eastern end of Lombard Street. In Roman times it continued to Bucklersbury, where it bridged the Walbrook, changing direction to west-north-west as it entered the Walbrook valley, east of the Mansion House. It ran beneath Cheapside, west of the tower of St Mary-le-Bow, taking a more direct route to Newgate than the present street by

[1] *RRB*, p. 195.
[2] *The Archaeologist in Essex, Hertfordshire, London and Middlesex*, 1959, CBA Group 10 publication (1960), p. 27, item 133 (i).
[3] Ibid., item 133 (iv).
[4] Ibid., item 133 (vi–x).

proceeding diagonally across it to the north side of Cheapside. Even so, its course was not quite straight, since there must have been a slight kink near the bottom of St Martin's-le-Grand to bring it to the line of Newgate Street, which it underlies. It left the City at Newgate, where a fine double gateway, about twenty-four yards east of the junction with Giltspur Street, provided an imposing exit after the building of the city wall.

Beyond Newgate the road dropped steeply to the Fleet, where it presumably crossed by a bridge. We do not know whether it took the straight route beneath Holborn Viaduct, which would have necessitated a sharp descent to the river-bank, or whether it changed direction on the slope of the hill; nor do we know precisely where it crossed the Fleet, which flowed beneath Farringdon Street. Roman cremations have, however, been found under Holborn Viaduct on both sides of Farringdon Street,[1] so it seems likely that the Roman highway crossed the stream very near the modern Viaduct. Farther west it must have continued on or near the line of Holborn and New Oxford Street. The latter, though a completely modern road and not the direct descendant of the ancient highway, is on its most likely course, and Roman burials have been found there. A lead cist, containing burnt bones and two denarii of Vespasian, was found in 1864 on the south side of New Oxford Street, near the north end of Endell Street.[2] A fragment of an inscription on a slab of limestone, evidently from a tomb near by, was found on the north side of the modern road in 1961, at the junction of Barter Street and Bloomsbury Court. This was from the tombstone of one G. Pomponius Valens, who was born in Colchester, and was probably a legionary seconded for special duties.[3] (*Fig. 10*.)

The road then proceeded on approximately the line of Oxford Street, although there is evidence suggesting that it did not always exactly coincide with the modern road. During excavations at the Marble Arch in 1961–2, a slightly cambered gravel surface was observed opposite the Odeon Cinema, twenty feet south of the southern kerb-line of Oxford Street, with its surface at a depth of about five feet below the existing ground-level. The surviving width was twenty-nine feet, and traces of it were observed extending over a length of nearly two hundred feet. Its alignment was east–west,

[1] *RCHM: RL*, Pl. 55 opp. p. 154 and pp. 163 & 164–5.
[2] Ibid., p. 165; *Proc. Soc. Ant.* (2nd series), II, p. 376.
[3] *Ant. Journ.*, XLIII (1963), pp. 123–8. The inscription is now in the British Museum.

46

Fig. 10 *Tombstone of G. Pomponius Valens,*
found in High Holborn, 1961, probably late 1st century

parallel with the modern road, but as the gravel was only a few
inches in thickness and overlay pottery sherds of the late second
century and later,[1] it presumably represents either the position of
the Silchester road for a comparatively short period in late Roman
times, or possibly the fore-court of a large building, such as an inn,
to the south of the road near its junction with Watling Street.

To the west the road continued on the line of Bayswater Road
and Notting Hill, where a change of alignment was made, so that
it took the most direct route to Staines, skirting the northern curve
of the Thames at Brentford, and apparently sighted on high ground
beyond the river near Egham. Its course is closely followed by
Holland Park Avenue and Goldhawk Road, until the latter turns
sharply to the south towards Chiswick. The Roman line is then
followed by two lesser modern roads, Stamford Brook Road and
Bath Road, and crosses Acton Green where it has been obliterated
by the railways. Half a mile farther west it is represented by
Chiswick Road, which leads to Chiswick High Road. The modern

[1] Information kindly supplied by Dr F. Celoria and Mr J. Ashdown, in advance of the publication
of their reports.

main road now follows its line closely via Kew Bridge Road, Brentford High Street and London Road—possibly even where the latter curves to the north in the neighbourhood of Spring Grove in order to avoid low ground. The Roman line is continued by High Street and Staines Road to Baber Bridge, but west of the Crane to East Bedfont the modern road apparently runs a little to the north of it.[1]

WATLING STREET NORTH OF THE THAMES

The main road to the north-west via St Albans (Verulamium), tribal capital of the Catuvellauni and one of the most important towns in Roman Britain, departed from the Silchester road at Marble Arch, and the present Edgware Road follows its course. Near the junction of these two roads, on the south side of Oxford Street near the north-east corner of Hyde Park, once stood a mysterious stone, believed by nineteenth-century antiquaries to be the 'Ossulstone' that gave its name to the Hundred containing London. This was subsequently dug up and placed against the Marble Arch, but it has since disappeared.[2] Although it was evidently of considerable antiquity, it was not necessarily a Roman milestone, as has been suggested, nor even of Roman date.

An old road-surface has been observed on several occasions during excavations in the southern part of Edgware Road, between Oxford Street and Upper Berkeley Street.[3] It consisted of flint nodules set in lime grouting, making a bed one to three feet thick. This rested on a foundation of rammed gravel confined within gravel concrete walls, which were overlaid by the flint metalling. The width of the road opposite Seymour Street was twenty-four feet. In places, however, the flint metalling was mixed not only with ragstone but also with small quantities of basalt and granite— stones that one would not expect to find in a Roman road in the London area. Moreover, there was no intervening surface between this metalling and the modern roadway. It may be, therefore, that the Roman road was represented by the rammed gravel and gravel concrete beneath, rather than by the bed of flint nodules. No trace of the southward continuation of Watling Street to meet the Silchester road was seen during the excavation in Oxford Street near the Marble Arch in 1961, possibly because the Roman road,

---

[1] *RRB*, pp. 84–5.
[2] *LAMAS Trans.*, 1st ser., IV (1875), p. 62.
[3] *RCHM: RL*, pp. 53–4; *Ant. Journ.*, IV, pp. 409–11.

which was apparently rising to the south, was here at a higher level and had been destroyed.[1] This negative evidence, however, inevitably raises a doubt whether the junction of the ancient roads was precisely at this point.

There can, however, be no doubt that the modern road to the north-west is on or very near the Roman line, since it is followed by a run of parish and borough boundaries, which are themselves of very early origin. After Edgware Road it is continued by Maida Vale, Kilburn High Road, Shoot Up Hill, Cricklewood Broadway, Edgware Road (Hendon), High Street and Stone Grove (Edgware) and Elstree Road to Brockley Hill, the high ground on which this alignment was sighted by the Roman surveyors. Here there was a Romano–British settlement of some importance, called Sulloniacae in the Antonine Itinerary. Several kilns were excavated on the top of Brockley Hill between 1951 and 1953, and these were presumably used for making the buff kitchen-ware found in great quantities on the site.[2]

Surface traces, apparently of an *agger* about 18 feet wide, have been observed just to the east of the modern Elstree Road between the Canons Park and Watford Way roundabouts.[3] An excavation on the supposed line in 1952, however, just south of the café opposite Wood Lane, revealed only a V-shaped drainage-ditch, 20 feet east of the hedgerow. This suggested that the Roman road lay beneath the modern highway; and old gravel metalling, 2 feet thick and $13\frac{1}{2}$ feet wide was in fact seen there in 1953, during an excavation for pipe-laying at the junction with Wood Lane. Moreover, another V-shaped ditch was seen about 20 feet to the west of it under Wood Lane.[4] There is therefore some reason to believe that what remains of the Roman road lies here beneath the modern highway, and that its drainage-ditches run on either side of the latter. Another old road with drainage-ditches lies about 30 feet to the west of the present road, but this is of very light construction, with a gravel surface on a causeway of clay, and cannot be the Roman Watling Street.[5]

On Brockley Hill the road changes direction to the north-east for one mile, swinging back to a north-westerly alignment on another

[1] *JRS*, LII (1962), p. 179.
[2] *LAMAS Trans.*, N.S., XI, pp. 173–88, 259–61.
[3] *LAMAS Trans.*, N.S., X, pp. 137–8.
[4] *LAMAS Trans.*, N.S., XI, p. 265, Site E.
[5] Ibid., Site D.

high point for a long, straight run to Verulamium. The course of
the modern road closely follows that of the Roman Watling Street,
but may take a gentler turn to the final alignment. The turn of the
Roman road probably lies just to the south-east of the junction with
Allum Lane.[1] It may be noted here that, contrary to popular belief,
Roman roads do not take the shortest distance to their destinations
regardless of obstacles, but tend to be laid out in straight alignments
placed with regard to the nature of the country, with abrupt
changes of alignment, usually on high points. In the case of Watling
Street, the line from Marble Arch to Brockley Hill avoids low, wet
ground to the east, and that from Verulamium to Elstree keeps
away from similar difficulties to the west. The short link between
the two alignments also avoids low ground to the west.

Watling Street in the City (originally called Athelyngstrate)
obviously has no direct connexion with this great Roman highway
of the same name, although, as we shall see, it may well be on the
line of a Roman street. Its western end, however, points to Ludgate,
whereas the road to Verulamium is connected more directly with
Newgate.

THE ALTERNATIVE ROAD TO THE WEST VIA LUDGATE

It is clear that another Roman road must have left Londinium at
Ludgate, crossing the Fleet where Ludgate Circus now is, and
presumably passing by way of Fleet Street to the Strand. Roman
cremation urns of the first, second and third centuries have been
found on the north side of Fleet Street, just east of Shoe Lane;[2]
and on the south side of Fleet Street fragments of a tessellated
pavement were found by Professor Grimes in 1953 beneath the
eastern end of St Bride's Church.[3] (*See p. 136.*) The Roman road
from Ludgate presumably lay between these two groups of finds
on or near the line of Fleet Street. It may be noted, however, that
Professor Grimes also found a wide Roman ditch beneath the
north-west part of St Bride's Church. This ran from west to east
and curved through 90° to the north, about twenty feet east of the
spire of the present church.[4] It evidently formed the south-east
corner of a large enclosure, which is likely to have extended across

---

[1] The Viatores: *Roman Roads in the South-East Midlands*, p. 22.
[2] *RCHM: RL*, p. 165.
[3] *JRS*, XLIV (1954), pp. 98 f.
[4] Ibid., p. 98.

the supposed line of the road. The ditch, however, was filled up by natural processes fairly early in the Roman period, and it seems likely that the road was laid out rather later. The purpose of the enclosure is quite unknown, but Professor Grimes has pointed out that the curve of the angle is too 'tight' for the ditch of a military fort.

Farther west, Stow in 1595 observed a 'pavement of hard stone' supported on timber piles, four feet below the contemporary surface, in an excavation on the north side of Fleet Street, between St Dunstan's Church and Chancery Lane.[1] It is assumed that the road continued on or near the present roads, and as the Strand is called Akeman Street in a charter of about AD 1000,[2] there seems little doubt that it is on the line of a Roman road. Moreover, the name suggests that in Anglo-Saxon times it was regarded not merely as a local road to Westminster, but a major highway to the west, since Akeman Street means the Bath Road. The same name is applied to the road from Verulamium to Bath via Cirencester, with which this road has, of course, no connexion. It is considered likely that it continued to the west on or near the lines of the modern Kensington Road, Kensington High Street, Hammersmith Road, King Street and Chiswick High Road, joining the main Silchester road from Newgate in Chiswick High Road.[3] It is clear that this road, with its series of short alignments, was not one of the original great military highways, but was developed from local trackways at a later date.

MINOR ROADS TO THE NORTH-WEST

This must also be the case with the roads from Aldersgate and Cripplegate. Aldersgate itself was a late Roman gateway, inserted after the building of the city wall, and did not therefore accommodate a pre-existing road. It seems likely that it replaced an earlier gateway a little to the north, which had originated as the west gate of an early second-century fort, the west and north walls of which had later been incorporated in the city wall. (*See pp. 112–13.*) Cripplegate was originally the north gate of this fort. Unlike the other gates of the city wall, neither of these fort gates was originally provided to give access to an external road that already existed: their positions were determined

---

[1] J. Stow: *Survey of London* (Kingsford ed.), II, p. 43.

[2] A charter of King Ethelred II, recording the boundaries of land belonging to Westminster Abbey. See *LAMAS Trans.*, N.S., XI, (1953), pp. 101–4.

[3] *RRB*, p. 58 and fig. 2, p. 55.

solely by the internal street-plan of the fort, which had to conform with the standard pattern. The typical fort of the early second century was shaped like a playing-card, and had a central street on its longer axis, divided into two parts by the headquarters building. In front of this was another street, which crossed the central street at right-angles, and ran right through the fort without interruption. A gate was placed in each wall at the ends of these two streets, and it did not necessarily lead anywhere in particular. The development of any external roads from these gates must have come later, and their minor character is indicated by the fact that they have left no obvious trace on the street-plan of modern London.[1]

THE NORTHERN BY-PASS

An exception to the rule that all roads in this part of Britain led to Londinium is found in a well-authenticated Roman road that by-passes the city to the north. It underlies the modern Old Street, the line of which it follows, and is attested by the discovery during a sewer-excavation in 1867 of two ancient road-surfaces, at depths of $9\frac{1}{2}$ and 11 feet, near Goswell Road. Roman coins, apparently unidentified, were found beneath the earlier surface and between the two road-levels.[2] It presumably departed from the main Silchester road in the neighbourhood of Bloomsbury Way, and I. D. Margary has suggested that it followed the line of Portpool Lane and Hatton Wall to Clerkenwell Road and Old Street.[3] After crossing Ermine Street (now Kingsland Road) near Shoreditch Church, its line is lost until it can again be recognized in the long stretch of road significantly named Green Street and Roman Road, leading to the ancient crossing-place of the Lea at Old Ford, where it joined the main Colchester Road.

THE NORTHERN FORDS

There is an indication of a more northerly Roman ford over the River Lea, between Hackney Marsh and Leyton Marsh. A gravel road was discovered before 1868, six feet below the modern surface on the east side of the Hackney Canal, 184 yards south-east of Pond Lane Bridge. Its direction was north-easterly, so that it would have reached the Lea at its S-bend, where there is now an islet—a

[1] For a detailed study of possible routes from Aldersgate and Cripplegate, the reader is referred to the Viatores: op. cit., pp. 117–25 and 185–201, with the warning that the suggested lines are only conjectural in the built-up area of London.
[2] *LAMAS Trans.*, 1st ser., III (1868), p. 563.
[3] *RRB*, p. 57.

place formerly used for bathing because of the hardness of the river-bottom, which would also have made it suitable for a ford. To the west of the Hackney Canal the line was formerly continued by a farm-road, now long vanished but approximately on the site of Rushmore Road. Immediately to the south of this, and west of the junction of Rushmore Road and Chatsworth Road, was found a fine marble sarcophagus of the fourth century, with the bust of a girl in relief upon it. (*Fig. 11.*) Now the property of Guildhall Museum, it can at present be seen in the crypt of Guildhall. The lid was missing, but the coffin contained a skeleton and there seems no reason to doubt that it was a genuine Romano-British burial. A coin of Gallienus was found nearby, and other Roman coins have

Fig. 11 *Marble sarcophagus with bust of girl in relief, from Lower Clapton, Hackney, 4th century*

been found in the neighbourhood.[1] The road apparently continued to the west, south of the Salvation Army Congress Hall to Clapton Alley, now Clarence Place. It may then either have joined Ermine Street, possibly via Dalston Lane, part of which is on the same alignment; or it may have turned on a more southerly alignment to meet the by-pass road near Shoreditch,[2] perhaps by way of Broadway Market and Goldsmiths Row.

The destination of this road after crossing the Lea ford must now be considered. Benjamin Clarke, who studied the topography of this district in 1867, believed that east of the Lea it proceeded in a

[1] *LAMAS Trans.*, 1st ser., III (1868), pp. 191 ff.
[2] *RRB*, p. 250.

E

north-easterly direction to the railway bridge, and then followed the line of Marsh Lane. If he was correct, Park Road and Farmer Road would presumably continue its course, but after this its line through Leyton Green and Snaresbrook is quite obscure. Margary suggested that it is represented by Lea Bridge Road between Leyton Green and Whipps Cross; and the antiquity of this stretch of road is supported by the parish boundaries, which follow it and continue its alignment to the east of Woodford New Road.

An ancient road might equally well be indicated by a more continuous straight line of boundaries, part of which is marked by Boundary Road, lying to the north of Lea Bridge Road and converging to coincide with it near its junction with Leyton Green Road. Both of these courses, however, are well to the north of a continuation of the direct line from the supposed Lea Ford, and could only be reached by a sharp deflection of the alignment.

East of the River Roding, this road meets a well-attested Roman road from Great Dunmow, and probably also another from Chelmsford. The precise position of the Roding ford is a matter for conjecture, but it must have been within about half a mile of the Pumping Station between Southend Road and Eastern Avenue.

THE GREAT DUNMOW ROAD

The Roman road from Great Dunmow to London is marked by a long, straight stretch of the modern road at first, and thereafter can be traced by shorter stretches of lanes and hedgerows as far as the Abridge–Theydon Bois road, where a short kink of the modern road followed it for about 150 yards, until the sharp bends were adjusted to gentler curves. There are no surface traces to the south-west of this, but layers of gravel have been observed in the river-bank where the alignment crosses the Roding, and again where it crosses a small tributary stream. This evidence must be regarded with caution, however, as it is possible that the gravels were natural deposits. The road then passes through the Little London gravel pits, where Roman pottery, coins, and evidence of buildings have been found. Making a very slight change of alignment, it then joins the modern Abridge Road about 550 yards north of Rolls Park. From this point it is on or near the line of the present Abridge Road and Chigwell Road, but where the modern road curves round Rolls Park, the ancient road continues on a straight course, and its supposed *agger* has been detected on the line of a hedgerow in the park. Others have suggested that it lies to the east of this, and is marked by a shallow depression running up the northern slope of the Rolls Park estate.[1] It leaves the Chigwell Road again when the latter curves to the west near the Golf Club-House, and farther south is represented by a parish boundary and by Roding Lane. This brings it within 160 yards of the River Roding, but we do not know whether it crossed near this point, where the parish boundary meets the river, or was deflected to the south, parallel with the general course of the stream and skirting its meandering curves, to a more southerly ford, perhaps near Red Bridge Station. A third possibility, suggested by V. F. Bignell, is that it continued on the Chigwell Road–Roding Lane alignment, leaving Roding Lane where the latter curves to the south-east, and proceeding in a straight line across the river, where it flows in an easterly direction, 200 yards north-west of the Pumping Station. There is no visible trace of it, and the river-banks have been concreted, so that any evidence of a crossing is concealed. West of the river, the same alignment is followed for a short distance by Nutter Lane, but there is no further indication of it in the present topography of Wanstead. To the south-west in Bush Wood, however, was found a linear earthwork, very similar to a road *agger* in appearance, on exactly the same line. A section was cut across it with unconvincing results, since most of the earthwork consisted of sand mixed with clay. An eighteenth-century map indicates a feature connected with the collection of water on part of this line, and it seems likely that the supposed *agger*, as it exists today, was made when the grounds of Wanstead House were laid out. There was, however, also a layer of compacted gravel and sand, more like the material of a Roman road, which partly underlay the deposit of sand and clay.[2] It is possible, therefore, that the remains of an ancient road were subsequently used for quite a different purpose after the addition of a layer of puddling. The coincidence of the alignment is certainly remarkable, and, as we have seen in so many instances, the position of a later feature is often determined by the line of a Roman road. The question must remain open, but it will be noted that, if continued, the suggested line would meet the Colchester Road just opposite the principal ancient crossing-place over the Lea at Old Ford. This is a more natural course than the abrupt westward deflection to the northern ford at Leyton. If it is correct, the latter route is reduced

[1] V. F. Bignell: 'The Roman Road from Dunmow to London', in *The London Naturalist*, no. 43, p. 78.
[2] V. F. Bignell: loc. cit., p. 81 and fig., p. 80, with correction in no. 44, p. 138.

to the relative unimportance of a branch road serving the settlement at Clapton.

THE NORTHERN ROAD FROM CHELMSFORD

Another probable Roman road seems to have provided an alternative route between London and Chelmsford. An excavation several years ago revealed a definite road-surface in the locality of College Wood, north-west of Ingatestone,[1] and a straight alignment of stretches of lanes and minor roads can be traced from Bumpstead Farm near Chelmsford to Navestock Common. West of this point it may be marked by a boundary on the same line leading towards Dog Kennel Hill. It would presumably have met the Great Dunmow Road at the Roding crossing.

[1] Information in a letter from Mr C. E. Dove to Mr V. F. Bignell, to whom I am indebted for drawing my attention to this road. See also *The Archaeologist in Essex, Hertfordshire, London and Middlesex, 1959*, CBA Group 10 publication (1960), p. 8, item 64.

CHAPTER FOUR

Roman Roads
South of the River

STANE STREET

The Chichester area was of considerable military importance in the early days of the conquest, thanks to the friendship of the local king, Cogidubnus, who wholeheartedly collaborated with the Romans. A supply-base was established at Fishbourne nearby, and recent discoveries suggest that there was a military encampment at Chichester itself. It is likely to have served as a springboard for such mopping-up operations as were necessary in East Sussex, and also for the advance to Winchester and the south-west of Britain. These tasks were carried out by the Second Legion under Vespasian, who must throughout have maintained a line of communication with his commander-in-chief and the forces operating north of the Thames. It seems likely that his dispatch-riders first travelled the route where the military surveyors and engineers were soon to build one of the major roads of Roman Britain.

Its line is followed by the modern highway along Kennington Park Road and Clapham Road, a straight road that points directly from London Bridge to Chichester. At the northern end of this stretch, however, the modern road curves along Newington Causeway and Borough High Street to the present London Bridge, whereas a continuation of the straight alignment would lie to the east of these modern roads and would lead to the position of Old London Bridge. There is some archaeological evidence that the Roman Stane Street did follow this line just east of Borough High Street. Gravel metalling was observed during an extension of the South-Eastern District Post Office and was found in an archaeological excavation on the site of 199 Borough High Street in 1945–7. Here it was in two layers separated by a burnt level, and beneath the gravel were two hard layers of sand and clay, which might represent road surfaces before the proper metalling of the stretch.[1] The road was not identified with certainty, however, in an excavation on the same line, farther north on the site of 199 Borough High Street in 1962.

The modern highway deviates from the straight alignment in a curve to the west along Newington Causeway, in order to avoid boggy ground where New Kent Road runs into the Elephant and Castle. The deposits of peat and silt are so deep here that it seems reasonably certain that the bog existed in Roman times, and that the Roman Stane Street made a similar deviation. A layer of gravel road-metalling, 1 foot thick and 15–16 feet wide, with a cambered surface, was observed in 1952 in an excavation across Newington Causeway itself, about 300 yards north of the Elephant and Castle.[2] It was also found, with its edge aligned due north up Newington Causeway, in a trench excavated immediately north of the Elephant and Castle Station in 1960. The layer contained Roman tile and brick, and was at a depth of 5 feet below the present surface, overlying the natural sand and gravel, so that it has been suspected to be of Roman date, and to represent the line of Stane Street, making the same deviation as the modern road.[3] If so, it seems to have rejoined the straight alignment east of Borough High Street to the south of the junction with Great Dover Street.

Clapham High Street diverges from the Roman line, which should lie well to the east of the modern road past Clapham Common. A gravel layer, just over 40 feet wide, with a ditch to the east of it, was found in 1967 in the playing-field of Henry Thornton School, on the north-east side of Elms Road. This was almost exactly on the line suggested by Margary, though not quite on the same alignment, and may well be the remains of the Roman road. Farther south, Balham High Road and Upper Tooting Road must be very near it, and Tooting High Street follows its line. The Roman road probably crossed the Wandle near the point where it is bridged by the A24, and there was evidently a slight displacement of its alignment to the west as a result of the bridging of the stream. Its subsequent line through Merton and Morden is not marked by any modern topographical feature, but it probably crosses Kenley Road near the south end of Daybrook road, and passes immediately west

[1] K. M. Kenyon: *Excavations in Southwark*, 1959, pp. 27–9.
[2] *LCC Survey of London*, vol. XXV, pp. 1–2.
[3] *LAMAS Trans.*, XX, pt. 4 (1961), pp. 170–3.

of Morden Station, lying mainly to the north-west of the present winding London Road, with which it coincides at the westerly curve of the modern road north of Morden Church, where evidence of its presence was observed in a sewer-trench. This at any rate is the alignment of Stane Street immediately to the south in Morden Park, where it was proved by excavation in 1958–9. Here the road was located in four places, in a straight line extending for nearly 700 yards, from a point north-west of Morden Park Cottages almost to Lower Morden Lane, near its junction with London Road. The road consisted of gravel, with a layer of flints forming the surface in one section, where a well-defined rut was observed.[1] To the south of Lower Morden Lane the Roman alignment converges on the modern main road at Stonecot Hill, on the line of the parish boundary between Malden and Cheam, which was marked by a hedgerow before the area was built up. Stane Street is then followed by the modern London Road through Cheam and along the western edge of Nonsuch Park. Through Ewell the present road departs from the Roman line, and it has been possible to check the position of the latter in several places. It was shown that the London Road alignment continued to a point in Church Street, just north-west of Ewell Vicarage, and that the road was then deflected to the south for more than three-quarters of a mile, changing direction again through Epsom to a new alignment, represented farther south by Pebble Lane, east of Leatherhead. This deviation enabled the road to remain on the chalk and avoid a stretch of clay north-west of Ashtead.[2] It may be noted that Ewell is rich in finds of the Roman period, and was clearly a settlement of some importance. At a distance of 13 miles from London Bridge, it seems the most likely place for the first posting-station out of London.

THE LONDON–BRIGHTON ROAD

A fairly important Roman road branched from Stane Street and led to the Brighton area, passing through the iron-working area of the Weald and the farms of the South Downs to some vanished harbour, lost in the sea to the south of Brighton or Portslade. It probably left Stane Street at Kennington Park, on the line of the modern Brixton Road and Brixton Hill. There is some doubt as to how closely it is followed by the present highway on its rather

[1] *The London Naturalist*, no. 38, pp. 22–3; no. 39, pp. 130–2.
[2] I. D. Margary: *Roman Ways in the Weald*, 1948, p. 73.

sinuous course along the southern part of Brixton Hill, Streatham Hill and Streatham High Road, between the junction with New Park Road in the north and Mitcham Lane in the south. Gravel metalling was recently observed in a sewer-trench near the eastern end of Telford Avenue, only very slightly to the east of Margary's alignment.[1] If this was in fact a Roman road, it confirms the view that the deviations of the modern road from the Roman line are very slight. Michael Green, however, has suggested a course farther to the west, based on a line of hedgerows and a track shown on a nineteenth-century map. This continues the straight alignment of the northern part of Brixton Hill to a point near Kirkstall Road, where it is deflected to a more southerly course, with Brancaster Road and the central part of Ockley Road practically on its line.

The alternative routes meet in Streatham Broadway, and the Roman street, after which Streatham is named, continues on the line of Streatham High Road, which deviates to the east of it, however, south of Arragon Gardens. The ancient road was found by excavation in 1961 near the eastern end of Hepworth Road, very near Margary's alignment, and here was about 32 feet wide, consisting of flint ballast laid on the clay, with a cambered surface of flint cobblestones and iron slag. There was a ditch on the west side and a small kerb of flint and chalk between the edge of the road and the ditch. Wheel-ruts, 70 inches apart, were observed on the surface. Farther south, it was again seen in a trench in London Road, where it was supported on a raft of hazelwood. The ancient ford over the River Graveney was also exposed by excavations at Hermitage Bridge, and it was observed that a layer of hard-packed flint and gravel, $4\frac{1}{2}$ feet thick, overlay the river-bed, extending for 100 feet downstream and 50 yards upstream.[2] South of this it apparently continued in a straight line, which is followed by the present London Road as far as Broad Green Avenue, where the London Road leaves it on a more south-easterly alignment. The Roman line is then followed by Handcroft Road and Pitlake to the railway crossing. Thereafter its route through Croydon and Purley is obscure, but farther south it can be detected near Caterham.[3]

WATLING STREET

We have left almost until the last one of the most important Roman

[1] Ibid., p. 118.
[2] *Surrey Arch. Coll.*, LIX (1962), pp. 88–9.
[3] I. D. Margary: op. cit., pp. 110–13.

roads, which is likely to have been the earliest—the great military highway, later called Watling Street, which linked London with Canterbury and the Roman Channel ports of Richborough and Dover. It is still in use as a major road, for the present road follows the Roman line most of the way from Dover to Greenwich. The last surviving alignment is the stretch of road, twelve miles long and almost completely straight, which extends from Swanscombe Park, through Dartford, Crayford, Bexleyheath and Welling, over Shooters Hill to the end of Old Dover Road just east of Greenwich Park.

The further course of Watling Street to the west is obscure. It is unlikely that it continued on the same alignment, which would have taken it to the edge of the Thames near the wide mouth of Deptford Creek; and it probably deviated to the south to remain on firm ground, skirting the alluvium like the modern road. The sinuous course of the latter, however, as it winds its way along Shooters Hill Road, Blackheath Road and New Cross Road, is most un-Roman, and it is difficult to believe that Watling Street is closely followed by these roads, although they may mark its approximate position. Nearer London Bridge the modern route straightens, and the line of Old Kent Road and Tabard Street may approximately represent the last stretch of Watling Street before it met Stane Street, just south of the bridge. It is most unlikely, however, that the Roman road corresponded exactly with the modern, and in Peckham apparent traces of it were found in the garden of 79 Asylum Road, and again in the garden of 59 Trafalgar Avenue, respectively about 500 and 600 feet south of Old Kent Road. It was found, however, that the road did not continue on this alignment, but presumably crossed to the north side of Old Kent Road, perhaps near the junction with Albany Road, where flint road-metal was seen during excavations for a pipe-line.[1] The change in alignment may have been due to the crossing of a stream near this point, and it is likely that the road changed direction again to converge on the line of Old Kent Road and Tabard Street. A possible trace of it was seen near St George's Church in 1964.[2]

THE LONDON–LEWES ROAD

This road, like the London–Brighton road, connected Roman

[1] *Surrey Arch. Coll.*, XLIII, pp. 68–72.
[2] M. R. Maitland Muller: 'Southwark—Roman Suburb', in *Guy's Hospital Gazette*, 26 December 1964.

London with the ironworks of the Weald and with the corn-producing area of the South Downs. It branched from Watling Street on the east side of Asylum Road, Peckham, where it was detected at a depth of 27 inches in the gardens of Nos. 85 and 115. It then seems to have continued in a south-easterly direction, which is not marked by any modern topographical feature, crossing the junction of Evelina Road and Arbuthnot Road, and lying just east of Selden Road. It would have crossed the railway line immediately to the east of Nunhead Junction Station, continuing a little to the east of Ivydale Road and approximately parallel with it. Between the two railway lines, in the neighbourhood of Nash Road and Turnham Road, were formerly the London Playing Fields, where the Roman road was sectioned before 1935 and found to be 20 feet wide, consisting of a layer of tightly-packed small flints, 6 inches thick, resting on a layer of large flints. The alignment would have crossed the railway line just south of the Brockley Way Bridge, and would then have passed beneath St Hilda's Church and across Guy's Hospital Athletic Ground near its western boundary. The road was sectioned in 1961 and 1962 in the north-west part of Blythe Hill Fields, where it was found to lie near but not beneath the slight hollow visible on the surface. This presumably represents a later track, which replaced the Roman road when it went out of use as the result of an earth-slip, apparently in the Middle Ages. The metalling consisted of a layer of rammed gravel and flints, 15 feet wide, with an average thickness of 14–18 inches, at a depth of about $2\frac{1}{4}$ feet from the surface. It was thickened at the eastern edge and abutted against a bank on the western side, possibly to prevent lateral slipping. A similar bed of flints was found in a trial hole in the south-eastern part of the park, suggesting that the road continued on the same course to this point.[1]

Soon afterwards, however, there is a slight change of alignment, and the road then runs parallel with Blythe Hill Lane, a little to the east of it. Continuing across Perry Hill in the same direction, it crosses the Pool River at the end of Winsford Road, and here there is another slight deflection of the alignment to the south. East of the railway between Catford Bridge and Lower Sydenham it crosses the Recreation Ground diagonally, and continues in the same southerly direction across the suburban streets of modern Lewisham, which bear no relationship to its line. It was sectioned before

[1] H. J. Vosper in *Darenthis* (annual publication of Lewisham Natural History Society), I and II (1961 and 1962).

the war at a point just east of the cul-de-sac in Meadowview Road, then in open fields, where it was found to be a gravel road, 30 feet wide, with very little camber, at a depth of 14 inches. The gravel was 11 inches thick, and rested on a layer of large pebbles and flints.

The road continues on the same straight alignment, now obliterated by suburbia, through Beckenham, crossing the railway line about 230 yards east of Beckenham Junction Station, and Manor Road near Downs Road, running approximately parallel with Wickham Road and between 30 and 70 yards to the west of it. It then runs through Langley Park, close to Langley House, and its gravel has been detected at several points on the Golf Course. Continuing in the same line, it crosses the railway just east of West Wickham Station, passing through West Wickham and crossing Corkscrew Hill, where its pebbles were seen in the hedge-bank. It was sectioned in the field to the south (Sparrows Den), where it consisted of gravel resting on broken flints and pebbles, which had been laid on a single layer of large flints. The line of the Roman road crossed Addington Road 270 yards west of Wickham Court Road. Sections were also cut in the fields farther south, just north of Rowdown Wood, and here the gravel was laid on a cambered bed of rammed chalk. The alignment follows the eastern edge of the wood, and from this point is clearly marked by the straight line of the Kent–Surrey boundary.[1]

THE PROBLEM OF THE WESTMINSTER CROSSING

Finally we come to a problem of great interest, which is closely connected with the origins of London and the relationship of the city to the Roman road system. Apart from minor by-passes, the Roman roads in the London area are aligned either on the southern end of London Bridge or on the town that developed at the northern bridgehead, with the important exception of Watling Street, north and south of the river. These two major roads, which must be of very early date, since they were clearly of military importance in the conquest of Britain, meet other important roads that lead to London Bridge, but point themselves to the neighbourhood of Westminster, where the river could probably have been forded without much difficulty in early Roman times. Were they in fact directly connected at a second river-crossing, and if so, does this mean that an important military route from the invasion beaches to

[1] B. F. Davis in *Surrey Arch. Coll.*, XLIII (1935), pp. 61–8; I. D. Margary: op. cit., pp. 124–30.

the interior was determined before London Bridge was built?

It is unnecessary to pay much attention to the fact that both roads are called Watling Street, since in Anglo-Saxon times Watling Street in Kent was called 'Caisincg Street', later becoming 'Kay' or 'Key Street'.[1] Moreover, as we have seen, the alignment of this road was in any case determined by the southern curve of the Thames at Greenwich Reach, which made a direct course for London Bridge impossible. The fact that it also points to Westminster may therefore be coincidental.

It is less easy, however, to account for the line of Watling Street north of the river and its position so far west of the City, without postulating a route to Verulamium that takes no account of London Bridge and therefore presumably antedates it. This is not necessarily inconsistent with the view put forward in an earlier chapter that the building of the bridge was one of the first actions undertaken by the invading forces of AD 43. The Belgic kings who ruled at Verulamium exercised political control over Kent, and had close contacts with Gaul, from which they obtained many kinds of luxury goods, including fine pottery. A route to Kent and the short sea-crossing of the Channel was therefore necessary, and it is likely to have been directed to the lowest point at which the Thames could conveniently be forded. This may well have been at Westminster, although, as we have seen, the easier and more popular fords were probably a little farther upstream. The direct route passed through woodland, and a considerable clearance must have been made to establish a track—a task for which the Belgae, unlike their predecessors, had the necessary technical and political resources. It seems likely that the Romans took advantage of this when laying out their own military road, no doubt improving and straightening the Belgic track as they did so. It is by no means unlikely that the earlier track also determined the general line of their road through Kent.

There is no clear evidence, however, that the *Roman* roads of Watling Street north of the river and Watling Street in Kent were ever directly linked by the Westminster ford. It is true that the fourteenth-century chronicler, Higden, describes a road that in his day passed from Dover through Kent, and across the Thames 'near' London, *to the west of Westminster* and thence to St Albans. Ambiguity arises from the fact that elsewhere he uses the same word

[1] *Surrey Arch. Coll.*, XLIII (1935), p. 67.

iuxta in a similar context meaning 'at' rather than 'near', and the phrase 'west of Westminster' could refer to the turning-point on the north side of the Thames—i.e. where Edgware Road leaves Oxford Street, to the north-west of Westminster.[1]

It has been suggested that Watling Street originally continued to the south of Oxford Street on or near the line of Park Lane, but no trace of it has ever been seen there, although a careful watch was kept on the many holes that were dug in this area during road-works a few years ago.[2] There is, however, a little positive evidence— perhaps not entirely conclusive—from the other side of the river, that the two Watling Streets were linked by a crossing at Westminster. It has been thought that the name *Stangate*, given to the old ferry steps north of Lambeth Palace, may indicate the existence of a paved ford at this point; and the eighteenth-century antiquary, Stukeley, said that a Roman road 'went from Stangate ferry across St George's Fields,[3] so south of the Lock Hospital to Deptford and Blackheath'. He also said that 'a small portion of the ancient way, pointing to Westminster Abbey' was 'common road on this side of the nearest turnpike'.[4] The turnpike is presumably the one on Newington Causeway just north of the Elephant and Castle, shown on Rocque's map of 1741, and it has been suggested that an ancient causeway may then have been visible in St George's Fields, leaving Newington Causeway near this point and leading to Stangate Ferry. Since Stukeley clearly states that a short stretch of the Roman road was still in use as a 'common road', we must look for an early-eighteenth-century road to the west of Newington Causeway, of which a small portion is aligned on Stangate and Westminster Abbey. The only road satisfying this requirement is the one that went from Newington Causeway to Lambeth, the eastern end of which is shown on Strype's map of 1720 pointing directly to Stangate Stairs and the Abbey.[5] After a short distance the eighteenth-century road curved to the west, but it is possible that traces of an ancient way continuing the first alignment could still be seen. There was in any case a tradition of a Roman road in St George's Fields, for it is also mentioned by Bishop Gibson in 1695.[6] If it coincided

[1] See *Arch.*, LXVIII, p. 232, and *RCHM: RL*, pp. 50–1, for the opposing viewpoints.

[2] *The Archaeologist in Essex, Hertfordshire, London and Middlesex, 1959*, CBA Group 10 publication, 1960, p. 98.

[3] The area around St George's Circus, then open ground.

[4] William Stukeley: *Itinerarium Curiosum*, 1776 (first published 1724), p. 119.

[5] 'A New Plan of the City of London, Westminster and Southwark', in Strype's edition of Stow's *Survey of the Cities of London and Westminster*, 1720.

[6] Camden: *Britannia*, Gough's edition of 1806, I p. 259.

with the eighteenth-century road to Lambeth for a short distance, it would have left Stane Street where the present St George's Road leaves the Elephant and Castle. Rocque's map, however, shows the turnpike *north* of this point, so that it is difficult to reconcile Stukeley's statements that the ancient road was for a short distance 'common road' and that it was 'on this side of the nearest turnpike', presumably meaning on the City side. Yet another position is indicated by a later observation. It is said that in 1824 a portion of the Roman road from St Thomas Watering to Stangate was discovered 'near Newington Church', well to the south both of the turnpike and the eighteenth-century road to Lambeth.[1]

More recent archaeological investigation has thrown very little further light on the subject. An excavation in Lambeth Palace grounds showed that there were artificial gravel layers, containing broken flints and mixed with lime in parts, that were cut by the medieval moat, and overlaid in one place by hard earth containing Roman pottery. The two sections cut suggested that the gravel deposit may have extended in a zone three hundred feet long and about forty feet wide, on an alignment pointing towards Newington Butts. It could be a Roman road, but there are several puzzling features. It had no obvious camber and was only slightly higher than the shingle subsoil. Moreover, its date is doubtful, since a stack of glazed roofing-tiles, not earlier than the fifteenth century, was resting on a surface only an inch or two above it.[2]

Farther east, in the gardens of 39 and 41 Cobourg Road, Camberwell, and in East Street, Southwark, just north of Alvey Street, a raised gravel ridge was detected running west-north-west and pointing just north of the Elephant and Castle in the direction of the turnpike mentioned by Stukeley. A section was cut across this line behind All Saints Church, Surrey Square, where a hard surface, like that of a road, was found, but the gravel was only three or four inches thick. This hardly indicates a major highway, and certainly not one that continued in use for very long, unless, as the finder suggested, it was the thin edge of a wide road.[3]

The evidence for a direct link via Westminster between the two Watling Streets is therefore considerable, but none of it is entirely free from doubt. If such a route existed, it would certainly account for

---

[1] Thomas Allen: *The History and Antiquities of London, Westminster, Southwark and Parts Adjacent*, 1873, I, p. 37.
[2] *Surrey Arch. Coll.*, XLIII (1935), pp. 76–81.
[3] Ibid., pp. 73–4.

the presence of Roman building material and a stone sarcophagus in the precincts of Westminster Abbey.[1] There is nothing to suggest, however, that in Roman times it was ever a highway at all comparable with Watling Street, north or south of the river, and it seems that the main route from the Channel to Verulamium after the conquest must have been via London Bridge and Londinium. It is possible that the earlier native track to the ford was given a metalled surface by the Romans and served as a minor by-pass. The ford, however, must have become increasingly difficult as the relative water-level rose and the effects of the tides gradually moved upstream. It may well have been impassable at high tide before the end of the second century, and even if it were replaced or supplemented by a ferry, the advantages of the slightly shorter route would have been more than outweighed by the inconvenience of the river-crossing.

[1] *RCHM: RL*, p. 148.

CHAPTER FIVE

The Status
and Functions of
Roman London

Our appreciation of the status and functions of Roman London has in the past been bedevilled by the somewhat one-sided picture drawn by the only historian who has anything to say about it. Tacitus, describing the town in AD 60, at the time of Boudicca's revolt, tells us only that Londinium was not dignified by the title of *colonia* (the highest category of Roman towns) but was crowded with traders and a great centre of commerce. He says nothing of its military importance as a strategic base, although this is implicit in his account of the remarkable determination with which Suetonius Paulinus, hastily returning from North Wales, pressed on at considerable risk with a small force in order to reach it before the rebels. His first intention was clearly to defend London at all costs, and it was with reluctance that he decided it would be over-rash to do so. The fortifications were evidently inadequate for defence by a small body of troops, though it is by no means certain that they were non-existent—an unwarranted assumption, which is based only on the remark of Tacitus that the rebels, who subsequently sacked and burned London, avoided forts and places under military protection. In the case of London the latter had been withdrawn, but only after a hesitation that implies that the place was defensible.

From this brief account grew the myth that London sprang up spontaneously through private enterprise, somewhat to the surprise of the Roman government, which eventually realized that the place might conveniently be used for official purposes. In fact it seems certain that here, as elsewhere, trade followed the flag. It is true that the Emperor Claudius chose to establish the capital of the new Roman province at Camulodunum, the ramshackle tribal centre of the great Cunobelinus, rather than on a completely new site. This was a natural decision at that time for a man whose sense of history was strong, and who was not noted for his foresight. It was at Camulodunum, therefore, that a *colonia* was established, and an imposing temple was built for the state cult of Emperor-worship, the visible symbol of imperial rule that distinguished a provincial capital.

At a very early date, however, the base on the Thames was found to be a more convenient centre for the administration of the province. The vital business of tax-collection and the control of finance was in the hands of the procurator, a man lower in rank than the military governor, but not under his orders, and responsible directly to the Emperor. The procurator Catus Decianus, whose rapacity triggered off the revolt of AD 60, was not himself at Camulodunum, since he sent two hundred men from elsewhere to reinforce the veterans who had been settled there. He was subsequently able to escape by ship, and there seems little doubt that his headquarters were already at London.

His successor, the statesmanlike Julius Classicianus, who, after the suppression of the revolt, persuaded Nero to recall the vengeful Suetonius Paulinus, thereby saving the rebel territory from complete devastation, died in office and his ashes were buried in London. A considerable portion of his imposing tombstone, one of the most important monuments of Roman Britain, was found re-used as building material at the base of a bastion in Trinity Place. (*Fig. 12.*)

69

Fig. 12 *Tombstone of oolitic limestone, restored, of G. Julius Alpinus Classicianus, Procurator of Britain* AD *61–?, found in Trinity Place*

It has been restored, and can now be seen in the British Museum, a noble memorial with fine lettering, which is worthy of a great public official. It was set up by his wife, Julia Pacata, the daughter of Julius Indus, a Gaulish cavalry commander who had played an important part in pacifying a revolt of his own tribe, the Treveri, forty years earlier. It is quite possible that his daughter was named Pacata in memory of this event.

The inscription is in two pieces, found on two occasions separated by more than eighty years. The first portion, found in 1852 with part of the ornament from the top of the tombstone, has the following words (reconstructed with the missing letters in brackets):

DIS [M]ANIBVS [G. IVL G.F. F]AB. ALPINI CLASSICIANI

'*To the spirits of the departed*'—a stock formula of dedication on a memorial to the dead—'(*and*) *of Gaius Julius Alpinus Classicianus, son of Gaius, of the Fabian voting tribe.*'

Roach Smith, the great nineteenth-century antiquary, correctly guessed that the inscription referred to the procurator mentioned by Tacitus, but his successors dismissed this suggestion, partly because it seemed too good to be true, and partly because they regarded London in the early years of the occupation as a mere trading-centre, unconnected with Roman officialdom.

The discovery in 1935 of a second piece of the same inscription, still *in situ* at the bottom of the bastion, showed that Roach Smith was right, for it included the title of the procurator:

.... PROC. PROVINC. BRIT[ANNIAE] IVLIA INDI FILIA PACATA I[NDIANA] VXOR [F]

'... *Procurator of the Province of Britain; Julia Pacata I[ndiana], daughter of Indus, his wife, had this built.*'[1]

A further indication that the procurator's headquarters were in London is to be seen on a wooden writing-tablet from the Walbrook in the British Museum. (*Fig. 13.*) This is branded with an inscription showing that it was an official issue for use by the procurator's staff:

PROC AVG DEDERVNT / BRIT PROV

'*issued by the Imperial Procurators of the Province of Britain*'

Fig. 13 *Wooden writing-tablet branded with official stamp of the Procurator's office, from the Walbrook*

[1] *RIB*, p. 6, 12.

Fig. 14 *Stamp* P. P. BR. LON. *of government brickworks on Roman roof-tile from Leadenhall Street*

Possibly also under the procurator's administration was an official brickworks in London. Its products were stamped P.P.BR., P.PR.BR., or some variant of these, usually with the addition of LON for LONDINII (*at London*). (*Fig. 14.*) The duplication of a letter in an abbreviation is often an indication of a plural, so that it has been suggested that P.P. stands for *portitores* (harbour officials) or *procuratores* (procurators). The latter is much more likely, since the procurator's department was concerned with a wide field of administrative matters connected with the financial and economic affairs of the province, and might well have controlled a brickworks for public building. If—as is most probable in view of the common variant P.PR.—the first abbreviation is the initial of an official title in the singular, while the second stands for PROVINCIAE and the third for BRITANNIAE, we have what could well be a shortened form of the title set out on the tombstone of Classicianus, and the claim of the procurator to the London brickworks seems stronger than any other.

An iron stamp in Guildhall Museum, with the inscription M.P.BR., evidently used for marking soft metal, such as gold, bears witness to the presence in London of an official exercising control on behalf of the provincial government over an important product. (*Fig. 15.*) The inscription is probably an abbreviation for

Fig. 15 *Iron stamp with letters* M. P. BR., *probably an official stamp for marking soft metal, from London, probably 2nd century*

METALLA PROVINCIAE BRITANNIAE—'*Mines of the Province of Britain*'—so it seems likely that the ingots from the Welsh mines were collected in London, where they were checked and marked by one of the procurator's departments before being exported. The stamp, which is probably of the second century, is therefore a further indication that the bureaucracy concerned with financial and economic matters was centred in Londinium.

This does not necessarily mean that London replaced Colchester as the political capital, but other evidence points inescapably to this conclusion, and suggests, moreover, that it did so at an early date. The symbol of the supremacy of Camulodunum was its great temple of the state cult of Emperor-worship, which was to be the focal point of the loyalty of the province. To appoint priests and raise the money necessary for the elaborate ceremonies and entertainments associated with the cult, a council representing the various tribes of the province was elected.

The provincial council met at the temple of Emperor-worship in the capital, where it elected the high-priest for the year and performed an annual sacrifice. It had to raise and administer a considerable amount of money, and maintained a permanent staff, which would of course have lived in the capital. A significant link with this establishment has been found in London. In Guildhall Museum there is a large hexagonal base for a statue, found in Ludgate Hill in 1802, with an inscription showing that it was set up as a funerary monument to a girl who died in Londinium and

73

Fig. 16 *Monument to Claudia Martina, wife
of Anencletus, slave of the provincial
council, from Ludgate Hill,
probably late 1st century*

whose ashes were buried in its western cemetery. (*Fig. 16.*) The
words are poignantly simple, but the bereaved husband who
caused them to be carved gives us in only seven letters a most
important piece of information. The inscription is as follows:

D.M. CL. MARTINAE AN. XIX ANENCLETVS
PROVINC. CONIVGI PIENTISSIMAE H.S.E.

'*To the spirits of the departed and to Claudia Martina, aged 19;
Anencletus, slave of the province, (set this up) to his most
devoted wife; she lies here.*'

Anencletus describes himself as *provinc*(*ialis*), meaning that he
was a slave of the provincial council, but although not free he
contrived to express his grief by means of an imposing monument.
He had evidently acquired some wealth, and his desire to com-
memorate his wife was apparently stronger than his urge to save for
his freedom. It is possible that he was in a specially favourable
position to get this work done at a reasonable cost, since the provincial council may well have employed stonemasons and sculptors

74

for work on the temple. Whatever the explanation, the bereavement of Anencletus has provided us with a historic document of great importance, which strongly suggests that London had replaced Camulodunum as the centre of the state cult—and therefore as the capital—at quite an early date. The style of the lettering is early and the formula at the end of the inscription—H.S.E. (*hic sita est*— 'she lies here')—probably indicates a date in the late first century.[1]

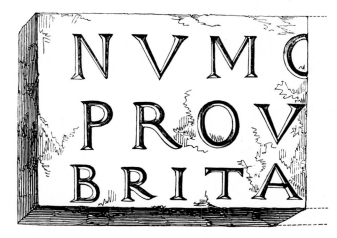

Fig. 17 *Inscription dedicating a temple to the divinity of the Emperor, set up in the name of the Province of Britain*

The reconstruction after the Boudiccan revolt would have been the most likely occasion for the transfer of the cult centre; and the subsequent reconstruction and maintenance of the temple at Colchester is no indication that it continued its former function, since imperial prestige demanded in any case that it should be rebuilt and respected.

The site of the great temple for Emperor-worship in London is unknown, but the existence of an imposing shrine for this purpose somewhere in the city, during the early Roman period, was demonstrated by the discovery in 1850 of half an inscription dedicated to the divinity of Caesar Augustus by the Province of Britain.[2] This was lost from Guildhall a few years later, but a drawing of it has been preserved in the British Museum. (*Fig. 17.*) The letters were

[1] *RIB*, pp. 10–11, 21.
[2]   NVM. C[AES. AVG]
        PROV[INCIA]
        BRITA[NNIA]
        RIB, p. 3, 5.

six inches high and the inscription evidently came from an important monument set up by the provincial council. The great stone slab on which it was carved was found in Nicholas Lane at the eastern end of Cannon Street, but had been re-used there as building material in a wall that was almost certainly of Roman date. The temple in which it was originally placed did not necessarily stand in the same neighbourhood, but was undoubtedly in London. It had evidently been demolished during the Roman period, and the inscription itself is of early date.

The close link between Londinium and the government of the province is also indicated by a fragmentary inscription on the corner of a slate tablet from Walbrook in Guildhall Museum. This commemorates Trajan's victory over the Dacians in AD 102 or 106, and its great interest lies in the fact that it appears to have been set up by the orders of another great imperial official, the *legatus iuridicus* (juridical legate), who was appointed directly by the Emperor to assist the governor by administering justice in the civilian zone of the province.[1]

So far no epigraphic evidence has been found of the presence of the governor himself in London, but other archaeological discoveries leave little doubt that he had his headquarters in the city. The use of London as a supply-base hardly accounts for the presence of a substantial body of troops there, long after the tide of conquest had taken the legions into the remoter parts of Britain. It is remarkable that seven of the sixteen readable funerary inscriptions found in London are military. This is a high proportion, even allowing for the fact that a soldier was more likely to be commemorated by a stone monument than a civilian of comparable status. As far as can be judged, these inscriptions range in date from the late first century to after AD 197—as is evidenced by the memorial stone of a married legionary in the possession of the Society of Antiquaries at Burlington House, for it was only after that date that non-commissioned ranks were allowed to marry during their term of service.[2] To these military monuments of London must be added the fine, uninscribed figure of a legionary soldier found in the Camomile Street bastion, and now in Guildhall Museum. This evidently came from his tomb in the cemetery nearby, and is likely to be of the late first or early second century.

It was early in the second century, also—probably in the reign of

[1] *RIB*, p. 4, 8.
[2] Ibid., p. 5, 11 (footnote).

Hadrian—that a large stone fort was built to the north-west of the city. (*See pp. 110–17.*) This enclosed an area of about twelve acres, and must have been intended to house at least one thousand men. A garrison of that size could have lived in considerable comfort in the fort which, if necessary, could probably have been made to accommodate twice as many men without undue overcrowding.

There was therefore a considerable body of troops in London at a period when its presence served no obvious operational or strategic purpose. The inscriptions suggest that it was composed of men seconded from the various legions, three of which are represented. Only one tombstone (uninscribed) of an auxiliary soldier is known from London. The Second Legion Augusta, based at Caerleon, and the Twentieth Legion Valeria Victrix, based at Chester, have two London inscriptions each; the Sixth Legion Victrix, based at York after about AD 122, one.

Although it is probable that the London fort was also used as a transit camp, it is likely that a principal reason for the military presence in London in the second century was the same as it is today. Troops were required in a capital for guard and escort duties and for state ceremonial, in Roman times as now. In addition, the Roman government of Britain was a military one, and the *legatus* was commander of the army, so that many administrative and executive tasks·would have been performed by soldiers rather than civilian officials.

It is significant that in the case of one soldier who died in Londinium, there is a reference in the funerary inscription to special staff duties. (*Fig. 18.*) A fragmentary tombstone found in 1843 in Playhouse Yard, Blackfriars, and now in the British Museum, is in memory of Celsus of the Second Legion, who is described as a *speculator*. This word, which is not unfamiliar in the modern City, had a very different meaning in Londinium. A *speculator* was in fact a kind of military policeman on the headquarters staff of the governor, and was concerned with the administration of justice, including the custody of prisoners and executions. Although enrolled in a legion he never served at a legionary station, but was normally based on the capital. He might travel in the course of his duties, but it is clear that Celsus died at his base, for his tomb was set up by three of his comrades, at least one of whom was likewise a *speculator*.[1]

---

[1] It is uncertain whether the abbreviated title SPEC. LEG. refers to all three men or only to the last named. *RIB*, p. 9, **19**.

Fig. 18 *Tombstone of Celsus, a soldier of the headquarters staff of the governor, found in Playhouse Yard, Blackfriars*

We have then good evidence of the presence in London of the governor's staff. What of the governor himself? Although he must have spent a considerable part of his time during the earlier period of expansion, and later at times of frontier disturbances, campaigning in the remoter parts of Britain, it is certain that he had a permanent residence in the capital, where he would normally have passed the winter. Until recently we had no idea where this was, but between 1960 and 1966 the remains of a great building came to light during excavation in the Bush Lane area, immediately east of Cannon Street Station. (*See fig. 19, opposite.*) It extends beneath the railway station, where massive walls and apartments with concrete and tessellated floors were seen, but not recorded, in 1868, when the station was built. Portions of it undoubtedly still survive beneath the railway foundation arches, and may perhaps one day be investigated. A large hall and a tessellated pavement were found on the site during the rebuilding after the Great Fire of 1666, and even then it was realized that the scale of the structures indicated that they belonged to a public building. The hall was believed to be the basilica, which we now know was elsewhere, but this was a reasonable guess, if the compartment was a large audience hall, as now

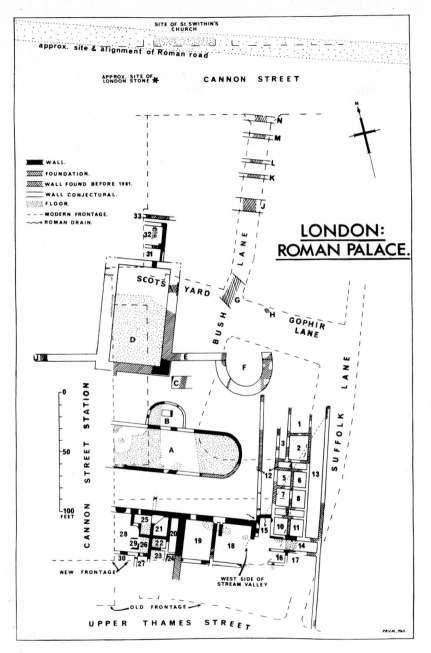

Fig. 19 *Plan of official palace, Cannon Street*

seems likely. The most remarkable fact, however, is that the mosaic floor was considered to be part of the governor's palace, a view that now seems likely to be correct.[1]

The plan of the building recently recovered strongly suggests that it was an official palace. To the north were great rooms, which could have accommodated a large concourse of people. One compartment, which occupied part of the site of Elizabeth House, and extended beneath the eastern edge of the station, was 80 feet by 42 feet internally, and immediately east of it was another room, apparently on the same scale, with an apsidal projection to the south. These might well have been state reception rooms and audience chambers. To the south was a central court, where a large ornamental pool extended for more than one hundred feet to the east of the station and for an unknown distance beneath it, indicating that the building had considerable architectural pretensions. South of this, along the river-front, was a not very luxurious domestic wing, possibly containing store-rooms and servants' quarters. To the east, however, the courtyard was enclosed by a wing of much greater interest, which, though not itself palatial, indicated clearly the official character of the building. It contained between two external corridors a series of fairly uniform rooms, some in pairs. The arrangement is not unlike that of a *mansio*, the building that provided accommodation in a town for visiting officials. There seems little doubt that this wing formed part of the palace complex, however, for its internal east–west walls were made parallel with the south wing of the palace, although the east and south wings did not themselves form a right-angle. This irregularity was probably due to the adaptation of a plan drawn up elsewhere to a difficult site on a steep slope. The partial conformity of the internal lay-out, however, suggests that there was a direct connexion between the two wings. It seems likely that the east wing, the site of which is now occupied by the northern part of Gophir House, accommodated officials of the governor's staff, and may have contained offices as well as sleeping quarters. The more luxurious rooms with tessellated pavements and painted wall-plaster in the north wing towards Cannon Street, seen during the rebuilding after the Fire and again two hundred years later when Cannon Street Station was built,[2] may well have belonged to the governor's private apartments. The official character of the building was

[1] William Maitland: *The History of London*, 1756, I, p. 17.
[2] *LAMAS Trans.*, 1st ser., III (1870), pp. 213–14.

further indicated by the use of tiles stamped P.P.BR.LON. from the state brickworks in London, which were found on the site in 1868 and also in the recent excavations. The use of bricks from an establishment that may have been under the procurator's control does not necessarily mean that the building had any direct connexion with the financial department of the province, although it was evidently a public building.[1] The Cannon Street site is in fact comparable with that of the *praetorium* at Cologne, which also overlooked the water-front; and the two buildings, though very dissimilar, have certain features in common. As at Cologne, there was rebuilding on a different plan, but we know very little about the later phases. The utilitarian east wing, however, continued in use with few changes for a long period of time, and here a considerable amount of dating evidence was recovered. This part of the building was apparently constructed in the last twenty years of the first century; and, since its plan was adapted to conform with that of the south wing, it is clear that the latter was already in existence, although it had probably only just been built. The east wing continued in use with only minor alterations until the latter part of the third century, when it was in a state of dilapidation. It was then occupied by squatters, who built a crude hearth in one corner of a room. Finally the floors were covered with a great quantity of dumped refuse in the early fourth century, when the wing was clearly no longer in use.

We therefore have in London an official building that appears to have been the *praetorium*, and this was apparently built in Flavian times. It seems likely that it was in this period that Londinium became officially the capital of the province, though it was probably the centre of the financial administration at an even earlier date. There was, however, a large and complex public building that lay to the north of Lombard Street and extended across Gracechurch Street; and this was probably occupied in the earlier Flavian period and not demolished until after the construction of the riverside palace. Was it an earlier *praetorium*, possibly dating from the period of reconstruction after the fire of AD 60, and perhaps the successor of a still earlier military head-quarters building on the same site?[2]

---

[1] These stamps have been found in various parts of the City, including Lambeth Hill and Leadenhall Street. Stamped tiles observed in a pier of the great basilica in 1881–2 may well have been of the same type. They have also been found in the military fort.

[2] *RCL*, pp. 137–8.

This building was deliberately demolished, apparently as part of a complete re-planning of the city centre for the construction of a great basilica and forum. The basilica extended from Whittington Avenue in the east, beneath Leadenhall Market, Gracechurch Street and St Peter's Church, almost to St Michael's Alley in the west—a length of about five hundred feet. It consisted of a nave separated from a northern aisle by a sleeper-wall with brick piers, which would have supported a colonnade or more probably an arcade. To the south was a similar wall with piers, one of which is still preserved in the cellar of 90 Gracechurch Street, beneath the pavement near the entrance to Grand Avenue, Leadenhall Market. It now seems certain that this southern sleeper-wall with its piers was the external wall in the western half of the building, so that the southern side seems to have been in part an open portico. At the eastern end of the basilica, beneath Whittington Avenue, was an apse, which would have contained the magistrate's tribune, and it is possible that there was a similar apse at the western end. To the north of the northern aisle in the western part of the building was a double row of offices, which extended across Cornhill. One of these was found beneath the Australia and New Zealand Bank, where a small portion of one wall has been preserved in the basement. A piece of the basilica wall survives also beneath the National Provincial Bank at 50 Cornhill, but for obvious reasons remains beneath banks cannot be visited. Evidence recovered from the site of 52 Cornhill in 1929 suggested that the western part of the basilica was constructed in the late first century.[1] The building served as courts of justice, town hall, and public meeting-place, and would also have contained the *curia*, or local senate house, the position of which is not yet known.

The existence of a basilica therefore indicates local self-government for Londinium, a town that Tacitus seems to imply had no clearly defined legal status in AD 60. He tells us definitely that it was not a *colonia*, the highest category of city, and says nothing more about its status, although he makes a point of describing Verulamium, the third town mentioned, as a *municipium*, the next category. The implication seems to be that the status of London was not yet defined, although its importance would have led the uninformed observer to think that it was a *colonia*. In recent times the City of London has been proud *not* to have a charter of incorporation; it is a city by prescriptive right, claiming seniority to

[1] *RCL*, pp. 134–5.

cities whose status was merely conferred by medieval kings. This claim to natural status seems to have been felt almost from the beginning, and for the first seventeen years of London's existence nobody seems to have considered it necessary to define its standing or to impose a constitution. The close links with the provincial administration may even have hindered the establishment of local government. This was a situation that the legalistic Roman mind could hardly have allowed to continue indefinitely, and the decision to make London the official capital must have underlined the anomaly. It is not surprising, therefore, that soon afterwards we find the city being provided with a civic building, which would have been the seat of local self-government. Since London was not a tribal capital (*civitas*), it must now have been designated either a *municipium* or a *colonia*, possibly at first the former with eventual promotion to the latter. In either case it would have had its own senate, which would have elected annual magistrates, the constitution being modelled on that of Rome itself.

Londinium continued as the capital of the whole country until Britain, for reasons of political and military security, was divided into two provinces, each with its own governor, after AD 197 but perhaps not before the reign of Caracalla.[1] It then became the capital of Upper Britain (*Britannia Superior*) while York, which now had its own imperial palace, was made the capital of Lower Britain (*Britannia Inferior*). This, of course, implies some diminution of the political status of London, but it remained the most important town in Britain. Under Diocletian further administrative changes were made, in which Britain was subdivided into four small provinces, each with its own capital and its own governor. One of these, the governor of the province called Maxima Caesariensis, was of higher rank than the others, and it seems likely that his capital was London.[2] The four provinces together, however, formed a diocese, at the head of which was a *vicarius*, who was responsible to the praetorian prefect of Gaul at Trier. The *vicarius* also presumably had his headquarters at London, which would now have served as a link between the provincial governments and higher authority, as well as being the capital of the most important of the small provinces. The centre of real power, however, had moved decisively to York, for military command was now separated from

[1] A. J. Graham in *JRS*, LVI (1966), pp. 92–107; but see also J. C. Mann and M. G. Jarrett in *JRS*, LVII (1967), pp. 61–4.
[2] J. C. Mann in *Antiquity*, XXXV, pp. 318 f.

civil administration, and its principal headquarters were at the northern capital.

London's status as the financial centre of Britain seems to have remained unchallenged throughout its political vicissitudes. The principal mint of Carausius was established there in AD 288, using the mint-mark L for Londinium, usually prefixed with M for *Moneta*. It continued in use after the recovery of Britain by Constantius Chlorus until 326, using the marks LON, PLN and P LON. No coins apart from unofficial copies were produced in Britain after 326 until another usurper, Magnus Maximus, was proclaimed Emperor in Britain in 383. Some rare gold and silver coins with the mint-mark AVG, issued by this ruler, are usually attributed to London, which had been renamed Augusta some years earlier. The older name evidently remained in general use except in official documents, since it has survived with very minor changes to the present day.

Our last glimpse of Roman London in the light of history, before it was veiled by the gathering clouds of the Dark Ages, shows that it was still the financial centre of Britain. The *Notitia Dignitatum* is a document that gives us the military and civil establishment of Britain in late Roman times, probably towards the end of the fourth century, though there are some later additions. One of the posts included is that of the 'Officer in charge of the Treasury at Augusta'. This Treasury no doubt contained both gold coins and silver ingots, like the one in the British Museum bearing the stamp EX OF. FL. HONORINI (*'from the work-shop of Flavius Honorinus'*), which was found in the Tower of London in 1777, with gold coins of Arcadius and Honorius from the mints of Rome and Milan. This small hoard is a sample of the wealth of Londinium in the last days of Roman rule, but it does not, of course, indicate that the Treasury itself was anywhere near the Tower. Still less does it support the myth that the Roman mint, like its modern successor, was in this neighbourhood, for it had ceased to exist many years before the hoard was concealed.

The importance of the financial and political aspects of Roman London, however, should not make us forget that it was also a great trading-centre, as Tacitus describes. Here came cargoes of the mass-produced red pottery from Gaul, with its fine, glossy surface and sophisticated shapes, to be distributed by cart and pack-horse so widely that there was hardly a farmhouse, however remote, that lacked a table-service of the ware. One of these cargoes on its way to London about AD 160, was lost by shipwreck in the Thames estuary near Whitstable, where the dishes and cups have often been dredged up from the appropriately named Pudding Pan Rock. From the Rhineland came fine pottery beakers with a dark, bronze-like surface, sometimes with convivial mottoes in white slip. Glass came at first from Italy and even farther east; there is a delicate bowl with exquisitely cut handles in Guildhall Museum,

Fig. 20 *Roman pottery amphorae found in London*

which, according to analysts of the Corning Institute of Glass Studies, probably came from the other end of the Roman world, since it is rich in antimony like the glass from Dura Europus on the Euphrates. Later, glass vessels of many kinds were imported in large quantities from the Rhineland. Silver and bronze table-ware for the well-to-do came from the Mediterranean, and later from Gaul. Wine was brought in *amphorae*, great double-handled jars, each with a basal spike for convenience in handling and storing in racks, from Italy and Gaul, and in barrels from the Rhine and Mosel. (*Fig. 20.*) From Spain came globular *amphorae* containing wine, olive-oil for cooking and lamp-fuel, and the fish-sauce that was indispensable in the Roman *cuisine*. Gold came from South Wales, copper from North Wales and Anglesey, lead from the Mendips, and iron from the Sussex Weald. Cloth and leather must have come to the London market from various parts of the country,

85

both for export and internal redistribution. A more sinister traffic is also likely to have centred on London. Prisoners of war were sold into slavery, so that during the period of conquest, at least, there must have been abundant supplies of British slaves, many of whom would have passed through the hands of the London traders. A leg-shackle from the Walbrook in Guildhall Museum may have secured one of these unhappy victims, although there are of course many other circumstances in which it could have been used. There is an apparent reference to the London slave-market, however, in a portion of a letter of the early Roman period found in the Walbrook mud, probably in Lothbury, and now in the British Museum. Written with a *stilus* on a wax-coated wooden tablet, the Latin words in cursive hand-writing have been firmly incised on the underlying wood, which has survived. The letter is a series of instructions, probably about the realization of an estate, written by a businessman of Celtic origin to a responsible servant, also apparently a Celt. It was sent to a London address, for the word *Londinio* is clearly incised on the outside of the frame, with part of a name. On the other side is the following letter:

> 'Rufus, son of Callisunus, sends greetings to Epillicus and all his fellow-servants. I think you know that I am well. If you have made a list, please send it. Look after everything carefully, and see that you turn that slave-girl into cash. . . .'[1]

The extent to which Roman London was a manufacturing centre as well as a centre of commerce remains uncertain. Not all of the tools and trinkets found in such great quantities in the Walbrook need have been imported, and Londinium is as likely a place for the development of crafts and industries as anywhere in Britain. The numerous finds of metal-workers' and carpenters' tools in the Walbrook may merely indicate that they were bought and sold in London, but no doubt they were also used there, and it is quite possible that some were manufactured locally from Wealden iron. Cutlers such as *Basilis*, whose name is stamped on the blades of several knives found in London, may well have worked there, though we have as yet no definite evidence that the cutlers' craft,

---

[1] Transcribed and translated by Professor Ian Richmond in *Ant. Journ.*, XXXIII (1953), pp. 206–8. An alternative interpretation has, however, been made by Professor A. W. Van Buren, quoted by Mr K. Painter in *The British Museum Quarterly*, vol. XXXI, no. 3–4, 1967, pp. 102–3. Van Buren suggests that the Latin phrase *illam puellam ad nummum redigas* should be translated not 'turn that slave-girl into cash', but 'squeeze the last farthing from that girl'.

one of the more important London industries of later centuries, was practised in Londinium.

Bronze-working was apparently carried on in the neighbourhood of Crosby Square, where crucibles, copper ore and copper solidified from a molten state have been found; these are now in the London Museum. It seems likely that small toilet appliances and personal ornaments of bronze and brass were made in London, as well as imported. Lumps of crude green enamel from Nicholas Lane in the London Museum collection may indicate that some enamelled brooches were made locally.

Goldsmiths were certainly at work in London as early as the Flavian period. In Guildhall Museum there are fragments of crucibles in which gold has been detected, found in a rubbish pit of about AD 80–90 that was covered when the east wing of the palace was built in Bush Lane. They had evidently been used in gold-refining, and with them were found pieces of the clay luting used to make an airtight junction between crucible and lid. Crucibles with traces of gold have also been found in a spread of Roman material containing nothing later than late second century, tipped on the marshes in Bermondsey, near London Bridge, together with pieces of a thin clay tube, resembling the stem of a tobacco-pipe. Its association with the crucibles suggests that the tube may have been a blow-pipe used in metal-working.

Evidence for glassmaking is inconclusive, but a great quantity of glass-slag and an iron mould were found many years ago with fragments of Roman glass vessels in Clement's Lane.[1] A much earlier record, however, leaves no doubt at all that pottery was manufactured in what were then the outskirts of the Roman city. Kilns were found in the brick-earth when the foundations for the north-east corner of St Paul's Cathedral were being dug, and at least one of these was full of coarse pottery. It is possible that there was also some attempt to imitate the fine decorated wares that were imported from Gaul, since, according to a later account, pottery moulds with 'Figures of Men, of Lions, of Leaves of Trees, and other Things' were found near by.[2] A piece of a rather crude bowl of this kind, which had been damaged in firing and is therefore likely to have been thrown away by its maker, was found in Aldgate.[3] Other pottery apparently spoilt in the manufacture, and therefore

[1] *JBAA*, 1st ser., XXXIV (1878), p. 254.
[2] Strype's edition of Stow's *Survey*, 1755, II, Appendix I, p. 23.
[3] G. Simpson in *JRS*, XLII (1952), pp. 68 ff.

presumably made locally, was found dumped near the bank of the Walbrook in Copthall Close. It is said to have included wasters of fine micaceous ware and black glossy ware imitating imported Gaulish bowls, as well as ordinary coarse grey pottery.[1]

Shoe-making and other leather-work seems to have been carried on in the neighbourhood of the Walbrook, where numerous scraps of cut leather have been found in the Roman levels. It is likely that the skilfully cut sandals and the shoes with elaborate open-work patterns, which can be seen in the Guildhall and London Museums, were locally made.

London, therefore, from an early date performed in some degree all the functions that were to make it pre-eminent in later times, and the pattern for its dominance has remained unchanged since the Romans centred their road system at a convenient point of entry to Britain. The strategic centre of communications became a great market; trade concentrated wealth, both in official and private hands; riches, together with accessibility to raw materials and foreign skills, brought crafts and industries. Except for a comparatively brief period in the general disruption of the Dark Ages, these factors have remained constant throughout London's history. The city's function as the seat of government, however, was dependent on the political unity of the country, and after the end of Roman rule this was lost for centuries.

[1] *RCL*, p. 229, 337.

The Roman City

The Thames in Roman times was wider than today, with the water's edge lying beneath Thames Street. From this the bank rose steeply to a height of twenty-five feet or so, and could be used for building only after it had been laboriously terraced. This was done by cutting into the hillside and by constructing retaining walls of stone or wood, behind which earth or other material was dumped to produce a level surface. Where there was any doubt of the stability of the underlying ground the whole structure was supported by massive wooden piles. The retaining walls of the lowest terrace formed river-embankments and quays, and have in the past been mistaken for a riverside defensive wall.

The river-bank was intersected in various places by streams, which cut small valleys through the gravel slope. One of these, the Walbrook, was a considerable tributary of the Thames, and into it poured a number of feeders, which drained the northern part of the city, especially on the western side of the main stream.

The Walbrook remained a dominant feature of Londinium throughout the Roman period and long afterwards, forming the western limit of the earliest settlement, and dividing the fully developed city in two almost equal parts. Even today its buried valley is visible where it crosses the modern streets, although its present contours are very much gentler than they were in Roman times. It can be seen most clearly in its lower part, in the great dip of Cannon Street, west of the railway station, and it will be noticed that the lowest point of the valley, representing the position of the stream itself, lies just to the west of the modern street of Walbrook. Moving upstream from Cannon Street, its course lies beneath

89

Bucklersbury House and the building of the National Safe Deposit Company. The dip of the valley is less obvious where it crosses Queen Victoria Street and Poultry, but can be seen near their junction fairly clearly if one looks for it—for example, from the corner of Poultry and Prince's Street. Continuing upstream, its course then lies immediately west of St Mildred's Court, and crosses Prince's Street near the middle. Here the dip is imperceptible, but the lowest point is marked by the modern drains in the central part of the road. These are directly over the Roman stream-bed. About sixteen feet north of the northern bank of the Roman stream, the Ward boundary is marked on the west wall of the Bank of England. It follows the course of the stream quite closely, with a few minor deviations, for the Walbrook and even smaller rivulets were still flowing above ground when the limits of the City Wards were determined, and therefore formed natural boundaries. An interesting example of this was seen a few years ago when a band of black silt, representing the line of an ancient stream, was seen passing right across a large building-site south of Newgate Street, immediately west of the boundary between the wards of Farringdon Within and Castle Baynard, which evidently followed its left bank. The approximate course of the Walbrook as it flowed in Anglo-Saxon times is followed by the boundaries of Coleman Street, Cheap, Cordwainer and Vintry Wards on the west side, and by those of Broad Street, Walbrook and Dowgate Wards on the east. The Roman stream followed in very much the same course, though it did not quite conform with all the sharp bends and deviations of the Ward boundaries. These may be due to the slower flow of the later stream, which in consequence was probably more meandering.

North of the Bank of England, the position of the stream-bed can be detected in the contours of the present road-surface, as it crosses Lothbury opposite the eastern end of St Margaret's Church. Continuing upstream, the course crosses King's Arms Yard and Tokenhouse Yard in a curve that takes it to the east of Copthall Avenue at the western end of Drapers Gardens. Another curve takes it across Throgmorton Avenue near its northern end, and beneath Carpenters' Hall. It entered Londinium just west of the bottom of Blomfield Street, and when the city wall was built across its course, an arched culvert was constructed to allow it to pass through.[1] Two other branches were similarly admitted by culverts in this area: one

[1] Two successive culverts were found in sewer-excavations in 1841 and 1837, at depths of 23½ and 18½ feet respectively (*RCL*, pp. 306–7).

entered west of Copthall Avenue and subsequently crossed this
street to join the main stream near Drapers Gardens; the other
entered in All Hallows Churchyard, London Wall, and passed
through the site of Winchester House, Great Winchester Street,
meeting the main stream farther south. In addition, several minor
streamlets flowed into the Walbrook from the north-west, draining
the area west of Moorgate and north of Cheapside.

The actual bed of the Walbrook was only between twelve and
fifteen feet wide, but the stream was subject to flooding, and
deposits of black silt have been found extending far beyond its
banks. These gave rise to the erroneous idea that the Walbrook
was a sizeable river, about ten times its true width. The stream-bed
was revetted with timber piles and planking in the earlier Roman
period, and may even have been navigable in its lower reaches at
that time for very small boats. The continued sinking of the land,
however, caused the Walbrook to flow more sluggishly, and this
early channel was choked with silt and submerged. The stream continued to flow, cutting new beds on approximately the same course at
levels that rose higher and higher as the land sank. The later beds,
however, were merely runnels, useful only as a source of not very clean
water and as an open drain—two functions that would not have
seemed incompatible to a Roman Londoner. Occupation beside the
stream was maintained as the relative water-level rose by dumping
earth to raise the ground artificially, a process that had to be repeated
again and again, as the land continued to sink. In the first hundred
years of the Roman occupation, there seem to have been few
permanent buildings on the banks of the Walbrook, but the
abundance of small finds and coins of this period in the stream
bears witness to great activity in the neighbourhood. It may have
been the scene of a great open market, in which goods were sold
both from booths and stalls on the land and from small craft in the
river itself. The silting of the channel, no doubt accompanied by the
flooding of the banks, seems to have put an end to this phase quite
suddenly, soon after AD 155—the date of the last coins of the
extensive Walbrook series, in which there is an unbroken chronological sequence until that year.[1]

The change in the character of the stream seems to have been
accompanied by a change in the nature of the occupation of the
neighbourhood: substantial buildings began to appear as the banks

[1] *Ant. Journ.*, XLII (1962), pp. 38–52.

were reclaimed, and the middle part of the Walbrook valley became a high-class residential district, with large houses from which came some of the best mosaic pavements found in London. One of these, found on the west bank of the Walbrook when Queen Victoria Street was constructed in 1869, is set in the wall of the old exhibition room of Guildhall Museum, now used as Guildhall Library bookstore, and unfortunately cannot be made accessible to the public until the new Museum of London is built. Another from the west side of the stream, found near the north-west corner of the Bank of England, is in the British Museum; and two others from the east side of the Walbrook on the same site are preserved in the Bank of England itself, though not in their original positions. One is in the private museum of the Bank, which can only be visited by special permission, but the other can be seen in the distance from the entrance hall (accessible during normal business hours) far below at the bottom of the main staircase. In the same part of the city, but about 150 yards west of the main stream, in a neighbourhood intersected by its small tributaries, and very close to one of them, is a small piece of rather inferior patterned mosaic, which still remains in its original position. It is preserved in the basement of a private office at Selborne House, 11 Ironmonger Lane, and can only be visited by special permission of the owners, Messrs Peat, Marwick, Mitchell and Company. The descent from pavement-level to the basement floor does not quite take one to the ground-level of the third century—the date of the pavement—and the mosaic fragment is seen in a well just below the modern floor.

A number of religious objects, such as pipe-clay figurines of deities, have been found in the neighbourhood of the Walbrook, and it is possible that the stream was in some way regarded as sacred. It is by no means unlikely that many of the coins, tools and other objects of some value found in its bed were deliberately dropped there as offerings to a local deity, in accordance with a common Celtic practice. The stream-banks would have been a natural site for small shrines, and we have good evidence for the existence of one of these. A dedication to the Mother-Goddesses, carved on a marble plinth, now in Guildhall Museum, was found in Budge Row, and this presumably came from the base of a sculptured group of the three deities that stood in a shrine nearby, probably on the west bank of the Walbrook. (*Fig. 21.*)

Towards the end of the second century, the important temple of Mithras was built on the east bank, very close to the stream, although

Fig. 21 *Marble plinth of shrine to the Mother-Goddesses*
'restored by the District at its own expense', from Budge Row

in this case the choice of a site was probably influenced by the need
for water in the ritual of the cult. Its position was immediately
beneath the porch and the main entrance-hall of Bucklersbury
House, where casts of the principal sculptures and inscriptions from
the temple can be seen. (*Fig. 22.*) The so-called reconstruction of
the building has been placed about sixty yards to the north-west
of its original site, on a terrace outside Temple Court, 11 Queen
Victoria Street. (*See fig. 24*, **7** *p. 99.*) This is really little more than a
ground-plan built from the original ragstone and tiles, and is not
an exact three-dimensional reconstruction. The visitor is advised to
see also the scale model in Guildhall Museum of the building as
it was found: otherwise he will be left with a misleading impression.
The structure in Queen Victoria Street has a curiously flattened
appearance, since changes in level have not been correctly represented; the door-step, for example, has been placed level with
the floor of the nave, whereas in the earlier phase of the building
there was a descent by two more steps to the floor. The alignment is
north–south, instead of west–east, and the position on a high
podium is almost the antithesis of the original low-lying site beside
the stream. Crazy-paving is used to represent both the earth floor
of the nave and the wooden floors of the aisles, and a wooden
water-tank in the corner of the building has been misguidedly
reconstructed with pieces of ragstone from the walls. Unfortunately,
many people are now under the impression that this modern 'ruin'
built from ancient material is either the real temple of Mithras
miraculously transported, or an exact reproduction of it, reconstructed stone by stone. Nevertheless it is worth a visit, as it shows
the size and general shape of the original building, with its buttressed
apse containing a raised sanctuary, and its central nave separated
from an aisle on each side by a sleeper wall, on which can be seen
settings for the bases of seven columns. These supported the roof in

93

Fig. 22 *Temple of Mithras, Walbrook, as excavated in 1954, view from east*

the earlier phases of the temple's existence but were later removed. Entrance was through a double door at the eastern end (southern in the reconstruction) from a vestibule or narthex, which has remained unexcavated as it extends beneath the modern street of Walbrook. This is not indicated at all in the reconstruction, although its side walls were found. The original door-step, with its iron collars for the door-pivots still in their sockets, can be seen, however, and this stone, worn away by the tread of Roman Londoners, is an authentic link with the past.

The Walbrook was crossed by bridge in two principal places: in Bucklersbury on the southern edge of the National Safe Deposit Company's triangular site; and just north of Cannon Street, west of the lower end of the street of Walbrook. There were no doubt other crossing-places farther north, which are yet to be discovered, and possibly another to the south, in the neighbourhood of Cloak Lane. These two bridges, however, led to the two principal streets of Roman London, which seem to have been laid out on the east side of the Walbrook in London's earliest town-planning scheme. Gravel was put down on the natural earth and rammed tightly to produce a firm, hard surface, which was cambered for drainage; and the roadway was repaired, when necessary, by the addition of more gravel to make a new surface, so that in time a considerable thickness accumulated.

The more southerly street lies beneath the northern side of Cannon Street, its modern descendant, and it no doubt continued into the western part of Eastcheap. West of St Swithin's Lane it has been found converging on the northern building-line of Cannon Street, and it evidently lay completely to the north of the line of the present street as it descended into the valley of the Walbrook. This road was laid along the top of the steep rise from the Thames, at the edge of a natural terrace in the gravel, the nearest place to the river where there was a long stretch of relatively level ground. The width of the Roman roadway seems to have been only about 16–18 feet, so that its southern edge would have been to the north of the centre of modern Cannon Street. On the southern side of the ancient road, and therefore beneath the middle of the present street, just to the east of Cannon Street Station, there stood in the Middle Ages a mysterious stone monument which, at least as early as the twelfth century, was known simply as *London Stone*.[1] There

[1] The first Mayor of London (1189) was called Henry Fitz-Aylwin 'de Londenestane', because his house was near the Stone.

seems little doubt that the Stone was standing in Anglo-Saxon times, but it remains an open question whether it was of Roman origin. By the time of Queen Elizabeth I it was deeply buried in the ground, with only the upper portion visible. In 1742 the worn stump, which had been for some time protected by a stone cover, was removed to the north side of the street, and in 1798 it was set in a stone case in the south external wall of St Swithin's Church. The church was destroyed by bombing in the war and the Stone was removed when the ruined wall was demolished in 1961. It was found to be merely the rounded apex of the monument, made of Clipsham Limestone and shaped rather like a tea-cosy. Apart from two grooves worn in the top it was quite featureless. It can now be seen replaced in approximately the position it occupied in the church wall, and in a similar niche, in the south wall of the Bank of China, which has since been built on the site—an odd resting-place for the last remnant of the ancient fetish stone of London. (*Fig. 24*, 8.)

Fig. 23 '*London Stone*', *photographed when removed from wall of St Swithin's Church, Cannon Street*

It seems reasonably certain that London Stone is either of Anglo-Saxon or Roman origin, but we do not yet know which, and we can do no more than guess at its original purpose. Since it is not a natural monolith, but a monument shaped by masons from quarried stone, it is unlikely that it is a pagan Saxon sacred stone, like the greywether menhir cast down and broken by St Augustine at Canterbury.[1] It was certainly not a wayside cross of the Christian

[1] This was found beneath St Augustine's Church, and has since been re-erected as a standing stone.

Saxon period, since in that case some memory of its origin would have been preserved in its name. Another suggestion, made first by Camden, was that it was a Roman milestone, perhaps the central milestone from which distances in Britain were measured, a provincial equivalent of the 'Golden Milestone' in Rome. Its Roman origin, however, has been doubted because it is of Clipsham Stone, an oolitic limestone which was extensively used for building in East Anglia in the Middle Ages. We do not know that this particular stone was exploited to any extent during the Roman period, although oolitic limestones from various sources were commonly used for monuments.

The man who had the best opportunity to judge the original character of London Stone was Sir Christopher Wren, whose views on archaeological matters were always sensible. He apparently saw the foundations, and was convinced by their size that the monument was not merely a pillar, but something much more elaborate, which he suspected was somehow connected with the tessellated pavements and other remains of a Roman building found after the Great Fire in the adjoining ground to the south.[1] These were undoubtedly part of the official palace described in the last chapter, and the recent investigations to the east of Cannon Street Station have brought to light a remarkable fact that seems to support Wren's view. The original position of London Stone, as recorded in Leake's map of 1667, was very nearly on the line of the central axis of the large hall that seems to be the centre feature of the palace. Immediately to the north of this great room was a small antechamber, and north of this would probably have been an entrance courtyard communicating with an imposing gateway. (*See fig. 19.*) These were probably all on the same central axis, so that the site of London Stone would have been beside the main road, either immediately opposite the centre of the gateway or actually in the middle of the gateway itself. It is hard to believe that this is a coincidence; and if it is not, the inference is that the monument later known as London Stone was of Roman origin—although the small fragment that is preserved clearly gives us no idea of its former appearance, and may even be a more recent addition to the original structure. The solution to the problem lies buried beneath the middle of Cannon Street, where some part of the monument probably still survives.

Parallel with Roman 'Cannon Street', and 136 yards (420 Roman

[1] C. Wren: *Parentalia*, 1750, pp. 265 f.

feet) to the north of it was the main east–west road of Londinium, which lies beneath the eastern end of Lombard Street, with its southern edge practically coinciding with the building-line on the south side of the modern street between Gracechurch Street and Plough Court. It was only about 20 feet wide, and so did not extend to the north side of Lombard Street. Farther east it runs beneath Fenchurch Street in a slightly oblique line, from the north side of the present street, east of Gracechurch Street, to the south side, just east of Rood Lane. From this point eastward its course lies beneath modern buildings, where its gravel metalling has been found on the west side of Mincing Lane, extending from 11 to 15 feet below the present ground level. West of Plough Court, also, the modern road has diverged from the absolutely straight course of the Roman street, the gravel metalling of which was found in cambered layers, amounting to a total thickness of more than 6 feet, just south of the frontage of 30–32 Lombard Street. The lowest level overlay the trampled surface of the natural brick-earth, and seems to have been laid almost at the beginning of the occupation of London.[1] Farther west, after a very slight deflection to the north, this street runs beneath George Street and the southern part of the Mansion House to cross the Walbrook at Bucklersbury.

Fig. 24 *Map showing the principal features of Roman London, superimposed on the street-plan of the modern City*

Things to see are marked with asterisks
1   City wall in G.P.O. yard
2   City wall, Old Bailey
3   West gate of fort
4   Intermediate turret of fort
5   Corner turret of fort
6   City wall, St Alphage Churchyard
7   Reconstructed Mithraeum
8   London Stone
9   House and baths, Lower Thames Street
10 Tessellated floor, All Hallows Church
11 City wall, Cooper's Row
12 City wall and internal turret, Tower Hill
13 City wall, Tower of London

[1] For a detailed account of the evidence for this and other Roman streets, see *RCL*, pp. 113–30.

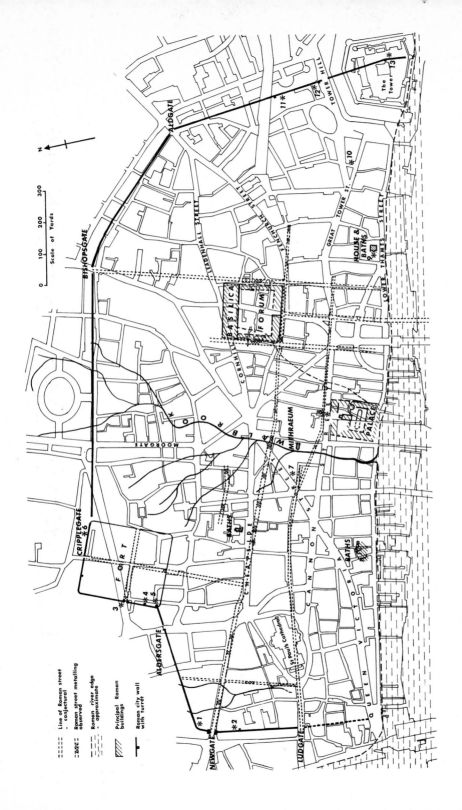

Scale of Yards

0   100   200   300

Line of Roman street
- conjectural
Roman street metalling
observed
Roman river edge
- approximate
Principal Roman
buildings
Roman city wall
with turret

BISHOPSGATE

LUDGATE

TOWER HILL

The Tower *13

*11

*12

*10

HOUSE & BATHS *9

FENCHURCH STREET

GREAT TOWER ST.

LOWER THAMES STREET

LEADENHALL STREET

BASILICA

FORUM

CORNHILL

WALBROOK

MOORGATE

MITHRAEUM

PALACE

*8

*7

W A L B R O O K

C H E A P S I D E

CANNON

BATHS

VICTORIA

QUEEN

St Paul's Cathedral

BATHS

CRIPPLEGATE *6

F O R T

ALDERSGATE

3 *

*4

*5

NEWGATE

*1

*2

LUDGATE

99

The area north of this main Roman street, lying between George Yard and Lime Street and bisected by the northern half of Grace-church Street, is the very heart of Roman London. (*Fig. 24.*) As we have seen, the basilica extended from Whittington Avenue in the east almost to St Michael's Alley in the west (*p. 82*), and seems to have been bounded by two north–south roads that were laid out not earlier than the Flavian period. The rectangle enclosed by these, the main east–west road and the basilica itself, would normally have been occupied by the *forum*, the business and civic centre, consisting of an open square, with porticoes, shops and offices on three sides and the basilica on the fourth. Very little evidence of the nature of the forum of Londinium has been found. Certain walls and brick piers found near the building-frontage of the north side of Lombard Street, immediately west of Gracechurch Street, presumably belong to the southern side of the forum, and these were apparently not earlier than the reign of Hadrian. The basilica that forms the northern side, however, seems to have been built before the end of the first century, so that there appears to have been a long delay between the beginning of the scheme and its completion. This may have been partly due to the presence, in the area required for the forum, of an indispensable public building, or complex of buildings, which could not be demolished until its successor had been built elsewhere. (*See p. 81.*) Perhaps by that time the first enthusiasm for civic building had waned, so that the scheme was shelved until Hadrian's visit gave a new impetus to such activities.

The pre-forum building is on a slightly different alignment from the basilica, being almost parallel with Gracechurch Street; and was aligned on a north–south road that was later replaced by the roads skirting the ends of the basilica. An even earlier building with foundations of ragstone is aligned on the main east–west road to the south of it, like the basilica and forum. The use of stone at what must be a very early date, together with its position in the heart of the early city, strongly suggests that this was also an official building.

West of the Walbrook, the main Roman east–west road does not correspond with any modern street, but runs approximately west-north-west converging on Cheapside, south of which several traces of the ancient gravel road-metalling have been observed.[1] It was first discovered by Sir Christopher Wren, who made good

[1] *RCL.*, pp. 120–2, 207 (**61, 62**), 208 (**64**), 245 (**192**).

use of it. When excavating for the foundations of the new church of St Mary-le-Bow, he had considerable difficulties, owing to the unstable nature of the underlying ground, where an ancient stream had flowed. North of the church, however, near the frontage of Cheapside, he encountered a 'Roman Causeway of rough Stone, close and well rammed, with Roman Brick and Rubbish at the Bottom for a Foundation, and all firmly cemented'. Here he decided to lay the foundations of his great tower, since the gravel metalling was 'most proper to bear what he had designed, a weighty and lofty structure'.[1] The position of the Roman road has therefore determined the placing of one of London's best known landmarks, a tower that stands well to the north of its church. West of St Mary-le-Bow, the road runs beneath Cheapside, and was evidently deflected to a slightly more northerly alignment, since farther west it underlies Newgate Street, which follows its line fairly closely, probably lying a little to the north of it near St Martin's-le-Grand, but immediately above it where it passes through the city gate to become the external road to Silchester.

In several places along its course between the Walbrook and Newgate the Roman roadway had to pass over minor streams. We do not know whether it crossed by means of wooden bridges—as it presumably did over the main stream of the Walbrook itself—or whether the waters were channelled beneath it through brick culverts. Two branches of a stream near the western limits of the city were very deep and must have presented a considerable obstacle. One small watercourse opposite St Mary-le-Bow certainly seems to have been buried, and the springs that fed it were used to supply the wooden water-tank of a bath-house that stood on the site of the Sun Life Assurance Society, 100–116 Cheapside. When the water-level rose as the land sank in the later second century, however, the tank was submerged beneath a pool of water.[2]

We know very little about the other Roman streets west of the Walbrook, apart from those in the fort, which will be discussed in the next chapter. Layered gravel deposits, which are probably the metalling of an east–west roadway, have been found in King Street and Old Jewry to the north of the main Roman street, on which it seems to converge.[3] There is evidence that the southern east–west road, which lies beneath Cannon Street east of St Swithin's Lane,

---

[1] C. Wren: op. cit., p. 265.
[2] RCL, pp. 204 (53), 205 (55).
[3] Ibid., pp. 203 (47, 49), 235 (154).

H

turns to a more northerly direction before it crosses the Walbrook, and continues on this line to the junction of Queen Victoria Street and Watling Street, where a cambered gravel roadway was found at a depth of $10\frac{1}{4}$ feet when Queen Victoria Street was constructed.[1] At this point, however, the road is said to have been nearly in line with the modern Watling Street, suggesting that it had again changed direction. It may be noted that the eastern end of Watling Street, beneath which this road is likely to have continued, is parallel with the main Roman street to the north, and these two ancient roadways would have been about 300 Roman feet (280 English feet) apart. It is also noteworthy that the east–west roadway to the north of the main street, between Lawrence Lane and King Street, lies at about the same distance from it. Although its general line converged on the main street, it could have been parallel with it here, so that it is possible that in this one small area there was a regular lay-out in the conventional Roman manner. If so, it was very limited in extent. The present Watling Street follows a gentle curve, which really consists of three distinct alignments. The eastern, as we have seen, is linked with a known ancient roadway and is parallel with the main Roman street; the central portion has Roman buildings immediately to the south aligned upon it; and the western would lead straight to the Roman gate at Ludgate if St Paul's Cathedral were not in the way. In spite of its un-Roman appearance, there is therefore a strong suspicion that the whole of this medieval street may be of Roman origin, although it has of course no connexion with the great military roads of the same name.

Another Roman roadway in this part of the city is a minor north–south road that skirts the eastern side of the stream south of Newgate Street. If it continued to the north of the main road on the same line, it would run beneath Greyfriars Passage immediately west of Christ Church.

The irregular lay-out of the western half of the Roman city seems to have been due to its rather haphazard development, and it was probably never as intensively occupied as the eastern half. Just to the south of the main Roman east–west street, in the neighbourhood of Queen Street, for example, was an area long occupied by a succession of wells, ranging in date from the first century at least to the third. No fewer than fourteen Roman wells were found on the site of the Bank of London and South America and seven on the site

[1] Ibid., pp. 125, 215 (92).

of Aldermary House.[1] It seems likely that here, readily accessible from two Roman streets, was a source of public supply in an open space. Wells continued to be dug in the same area in the Middle Ages and later, and the small alley to the north of Aldermary House is still called by its seventeenth-century name of Well Court. The Roman wells were timber-lined—either square, with a box-like frame of oak planks, or round, with a frame of pine-wood barrels placed one above the other.

Farther west, in the neighbourhood of St Martin's-le-Grand and St Paul's Cathedral were undeveloped districts where the brick-earth was dug to make tiles and pots, and where cremation urns of the earlier Roman period were buried—a certain indication that the area was then unoccupied by houses. To the south of Cannon Street, near its western end, gravel was quarried for road-making and the surfacing of courtyards. Here as elsewhere, the holes dug for gravel and brick-earth and wells that had become useless through silting were subsequently used as dumping places for refuse. Only farther south near the water-front in this part of Londinium are there indications of important buildings—a massive structure, not yet identified, built on terraces at Lambeth Hill[2] and a public bath-house set into the rising ground at Huggin Hill.[3]

The latter was apparently built in the Flavian period, when such governors as Agricola were pursuing an active policy of civilizing the Britons by teaching them the ways of their conquerors. The daily visit to the baths, more than anything else, gave its distinctive flavour to Roman city life, providing sport, physical pleasure, relaxation, gossip and the opportunities for intrigue. After taking exercise the bather entered various hot-rooms to induce perspiration, usually splashing himself with hot water from a large tub. He then cooled off in a colder room, and could finish by taking a cold plunge. Essential equipment for visiting the baths were a curved scraper of iron or bronze, called a strigil, for rubbing down the body, and a small glass flask of scented oil used for replacing the natural oils lost by perspiration. Examples of both can be seen in Guildhall and London Museums. (*Fig. 25.*)

A considerable part of the hot-room of the Huggin Hill bath-house still survives, buried beneath the courtyard east of Dominant House, 205 Upper Thames Street. If sufficient money for the

[1] Ibid., pp. 214 (89), 215 (91).
[2] Ibid., pp. 220–2 (110–114).
[3] Ibid., p. 141, fig. 26, and p. 142; *LAMAS Trans.*, XXI, pt. 3 (1967), pp. 194–202.

Fig. 25 *Roman iron strigil and glass oil-flask used in the baths, found in London*

purpose were available, it might be possible for it to be made permanently accessible to the public in an inspection chamber, without interfering with the use of the courtyard, but nothing can be seen at present. In January 1969, however, a piece of the great Roman retaining wall to the north of it remains visible on the southern edge of the adjoining site farther up the hill. It is built of ragstone, with a double course of bonding-tiles near the top, and is faced on the southern side with *opus signinum*, the characteristic Roman concrete that contains broken tile.

A portion of the warm-room of another Roman bath-house has long been preserved in Lower Thames Street, in the eastern part of the city. It occupies a similar position near the bottom of the steep bank rising from the river, just east of St Mary-at-Hill, on the site formerly occupied by the Coal Exchange. Although it is not at present normally open to the public, arrangements to visit it can be made with the Director of Guildhall Museum. It shows clearly the Roman method of central heating by means of a hypocaust. The concrete floor is raised on brick pillars, making a space below through which hot air from the furnace was circulated. A brick seat for the bathers, forming part of a partition wall, can also be seen. Unlike the bath-house in Upper Thames Street, which seems to have been demolished in the first half of the second century, this one was in use in later Roman times, and the building itself seems to have been occupied until the very end of the Roman period. The small size of the heated chambers shows that it was a private bath-house in a large mansion, part of which has been found.

Fig. 26 *Hot-room of Roman bath-house from the west,
as excavated in 1968, showing the tile* pilae *that supported
the vanished floor. The hot air passed from a
furnace through the curved wall on the right, under
the floor and up through the flue-tiles in the nearer wall.
On the right is an unheated room with a tessellated floor*

Excavations in 1968 have uncovered the hot-room to the east and a
cold-room with a plain tessellated floor to the south. (*Fig. 26.*) It
is hoped to preserve these also, and to make them accessible to the
public in due course. (*Fig. 24, 9, p. 99.*)

Plunge-baths alone have been recorded in the western part of
Cannon Street and in Threadneedle Street.[1] It should be noted,
however, that the modern Roman Bath Street, west of St Martin's-
le-Grand, has no connexion with any discovery of ancient baths,
but is named after a *bagnio* of the eighteenth century.

We do not know very much about the topography of the eastern
end of the city, but Roman buildings extended as far as the Tower
of London. The red tessellated floor of a house can still be seen in
its original position beneath the tower of All Hallows Barking

[1] *RCL*, pp. 214 (86), 243 (182).

Church,[1] near the bottom of the stairway to the crypt. (*Fig. 24,* **10.**) It is divided by a gully marking the position of a wooden partition wall, and part of a moulding in pink plaster with a light red surface can be seen at the junction of the floor and the partition. A small piece of a similar floor of coarse red tesserae has been set in recent years in the floor of the crypt farther east, below the level at which it was found. Roman walls of ragstone and flint with a course of bonding-tiles, forming three sides of a room or corridor, were found beneath the central part of the church, and a section of one can be seen in the north wall of the crypt. They were on the same alignment as the floor and partition wall under the tower, and probably formed part of the same building, since both portions were built not earlier than the late second century. Before that date the site seems to have been occupied by plastered timber houses.[2] The alignment of the later Roman building is the same as that of the present tower, which is set askew to the main body of the church and is parallel to Great Tower Street, which may follow the line of a Roman street.

Access to the crypt can be obtained on application to the verger, and it is well worth a visit, not only for the sake of its Roman pavement, but also for the other exhibits that it contains. The most notable are the fragments of carved Anglo-Saxon crosses found in the church, but there are also a large model of Roman London— reconstructed with buildings that are necessarily mostly imaginary[3] —and finds of the Roman period, not all of them from this site. A word of warning is necessary here: the striking tombstone with the Greek inscription was found at Tilbury, and has been claimed as a find from the eastern cemetery of Roman London, dumped on the Essex marshes with material excavated when the Underground Railway was built from Tower Hill to Aldgate. It is of imported marble, however, probably from the Greek islands, and is not generally accepted by scholars as a tombstone of Roman Britain. It was almost certainly brought home by an English gentleman making the Grand Tour in the last 350 years.

A typical sculpture of Roman Britain, which was found about

[1] West of the Tower of London.
[2] *RCL*, pp. 296–7 (358, 359).
[3] A printed key to this model has been prepared, and it must be strongly emphasized that *this is in no sense a map of Roman London.* The model was constructed many years ago and, although some revisions have been made, other details are now known to be quite incorrect. Many of the most striking features (e.g. the theatre) are not only imaginary, but certainly did not exist where they are shown.

170 yards north of this site, near the church of St Olave Hart Street, is represented by a cast in All Hallows crypt, and the original can be seen in Guildhall Museum. This is a large group (unfortunately incomplete, with the heads missing) representing the three Celtic Mother-Goddesses, seated, each with a basket of fruit on her lap. It was found during sewer-excavations more than a hundred years ago, and is said to have been lying on a Roman pavement. Its size and weight make it unlikely that it was moved far from its original position, which was evidently in a shrine or temple. This presumably stood somewhere near the junction of Seething Lane and Hart Street.

The Roman city did not lack imposing monuments and statues, but only a few fragments have survived.[1] The finest is the great bronze head of Hadrian, dredged from the Thames near London Bridge in 1834, and now in the British Museum. (*Fig. 27.*) The

Fig. 27 *Bronze head of the Emperor Hadrian, from the Thames near London Bridge*

[1] It is perhaps necessary to mention that the statue of a Roman Emperor in the garden near the city wall on Tower Hill is a 19th-century composite figure, with the head of Trajan and the body of Augustus, and has nothing to do with Roman London.

figure from which it came was larger than life-size, and must originally have stood in a prominent position, perhaps in the forum itself. A bronze hand found in Lower Thames Street is also in the British Museum. Since it is on a similar scale and presumably also came from the river-bed, which underlies the southern half of Thames Street, it may well have belonged to the same statue. We can only speculate on the train of events that brought significant fragments of a great figure of imperial might, not to the melting-pot, as might be expected, but to a resting-place in London's river. Did some vestige of awe or superstitious fear save them from the normal fate of scrap metal, or did some memory of sacrificial offerings to the Thames last longer than respect for a pagan Emperor? It is unlikely that we shall ever know.

Two other hands from large Roman bronze statues are in Guildhall Museum—one from Gracechurch Street, and the other found in a well east of Seething Lane (a circumstance that might also suggest the idea of a votive offering). A stone head larger than life-size, found in the filling of a bastion of the city wall in Camomile Street, and now in Guildhall Museum, may be from a statue of a third century Emperor—Philip I or Trajan Decius—though it is equally possible that it comes from a large funerary monument of that date.[1]

The imperial statues of Roman London would no doubt have stood on tall plinths, or even columns, and it used to be thought that a great Roman column base, preserved in the crypt at Guildhall, originally formed part of one of these monuments. It is of Egyptian granite, however, and there seems no doubt that it is the granite 'bowl' that was sent home from Alexandria by Major (later General) George Cookson in 1802. He presented it to the City as 'a memorial of British achievements in Egypt', where he had been in command of the artillery, and it has since remained unlabelled and unrecorded in Guildhall crypt.[2] No living person seems to have seen the under-side of this huge piece of stone, but it is presumably hollow, as it was thought to be a bowl. Its true nature was evidently realized and it was turned the right way up, only to mystify and mislead subsequent generations of archaeologists, who could not believe that anyone would have brought home in recent times a mere column base of such massive proportions (more than $5\frac{1}{2}$ feet wide at the

[1] J. M. C. Toynbee: *Art in Britain under the Romans*, 1964, p. 55.
[2] *Illustrated News*, 24 May 1851, pp. 467–8; J. Timbs: *Curiosities of London*, 1855, p. 301.

bottom). It was therefore long thought to be a genuine relic of Roman London.[1]

There is suspicion also about a sculptured marble fragment in purely classical style in Guildhall Museum, and therefore presumably found in London, though without a recorded find-spot. It is part of a scene in relief representing the Rape of the Sabine Women, presumably one of a series illustrating the legendary history of Rome, which probably decorated a public building. This may have stood in Londinium, which we know possessed great buildings worthy of ornamentation with imported works of art, but it is as likely that it was brought from the Mediterranean in more recent times.

Excluding such doubtful testimony, we can build up from the scattered and fragmentary evidence a picture of a city of marked contrasts. Metropolitan splendour was never far removed from a squalor that was rustic rather than slummy. There was no lack of space for a population that probably never exceeded 50,000, and parts of the 330 acres within the city walls were sparsely occupied or even left as open spaces. Londinium had its government and civic buildings, its public baths and mansions with mosaic pavements and central heating, built of masonry and brick, often with roofs of overlapping tiles of the kind familiar to all visitors to Mediterranean countries; it also had its humbler dwellings of wood, wattle and daub, and even unbaked clay, with earth floors and thatched roofs. Combinations of the richer and poorer materials were often to be seen in different parts of the same building, and even the humblest households often covered the poverty of their walls with painted plaster.

[1] *RCHM : RL*, pp. 42–3.

 *The Fortifications of Roman London*

It is likely that the earliest London was provided with earthwork defences, consisting of a ditch with palisaded rampart, but we can only guess at their probable position. They would presumably have enclosed the early nucleus of London on the east side of the Walbrook, and would have protected the bridgehead. It can be assumed that they disappeared at an early date, perhaps even before the revolt of Boudicca, and their traces would be difficult to detect in a builders' excavation. The only indication of their probable existence and approximate position is an irregularity in the street-plan: the main east–west street on the east of the Walbrook makes a sharp angle with the road to Colchester in the east, and does not point straight at the Walbrook bridge on the west. It seems, therefore, to be the *decumanus maximus* of a planned settlement of even earlier date than the permanent road to the first capital and the bridging of the Walbrook. The fortifications were presumably at the limits of this nucleus, so that their eastern and western lines are likely to have been at the ends of the straight stretch of the roadway. We do not yet know precisely where these were, but the eastern end must have been east of Mincing Lane, and the western to the west of Clement's Lane.[1] Further discoveries showing the exact course of this street east of the Walbrook offer the best hope of defining the limits of the first settlement and the position of its probable fortifications.

THE EARLY-SECOND-CENTURY FORT

Fairly early in the second century, but at a date that may prove

[1] Immediately west of Clement's Lane there may also have been a kink in the road where it crossed a stream (filled in before A.D. 100).

to be in the reign of Hadrian rather than Trajan, a stone fort was built in the north-western part of the city, in an area that had hitherto been very sparsely occupied. It was of the standard playing-card shape—rectangular with rounded corners—and had the standard lay-out of internal streets—an east–west street placed off-centre and running straight through the fort, and a north–south street at right-angles to this on the central axis, divided into two parts by the headquarters building to which it led. These features have left a lasting mark on the topography of the City of London. The north and west walls formed part of the later city wall, and determined the curious course of the latter with its re-entrant east of Aldersgate. The internal streets survived, with slight divergences from their original lines, until modern times.

The north–south street of the central axis is represented by the northern part of Wood Street, which leads to Cripplegate, the only gateway of the city that is not represented now by a busy thorough-fare. It has always given access only to minor roads, although it is now known to be the oldest gate of all, antedating the city wall itself. With the exception of Aldersgate, which seems to have been an afterthought, the other Roman gates were made when the wall was built, to accommodate pre-existing roads. Cripplegate was already there, and owed its existence solely to the fact that a military fort built to the standard pattern had to have a gate at each end of its central axis. The corresponding gate to the south lay near the south wall of 100, Wood Street, just west of the modern street, which deviates slightly to the east of its Roman predecessor in the southern part of the fort.

The west and north sides of the fort are indicated by the line of the later city wall, which forms a right-angle at the medieval corner-bastion south-west of St Giles's Church. The east side was located in a recent excavation, immediately east of Aldermanbury, in the car-park to the west of Guildhall, and a little farther north it lies beneath the roadway of Aldermanbury.

The approximate position of the east–west street of the fort was marked until very recently by two modern streets, Silver Street and Addle Street, although the eastern part of the latter curved to the north of its line. Of these streets, survivals of the medieval and, as is now apparent, the Roman street-plan, only the western end of Addle Street remains near its original place. Silver Street has disappeared in the post-war reconstruction, and the shape of the rest of Addle Street has been further distorted into an S-bend, well to the north of the Roman street.

Beneath the new highway of London Wall the remains of the northern half of the west gate of the fort have been preserved, in a separate compartment at the western end of the underground car-park, and can be visited free of charge between 12.30 and 2 p.m., Monday to Friday—except on Bank Holidays. (*See fig. 24,* **3**.) Visits for organized parties can often be arranged at other times by application a week or two in advance to the Director of Guildhall Museum. Entrance is from the north side of the double carriage-way of London Wall, south of the medieval bastion. The visitor descends a flight of steps that take him beneath the modern road, and a door on the right gives access to the remains of the fort gate, of which only the lower portions of the walls survive. He turns after entering the compartment, so that he is looking to the east and standing just outside the gate, approximately at Roman ground-level. On his right he will see two piers of masonry, which were at the centre of the double gate. From each once sprang a double archway, and from the viewpoint of the visitor it would have been possible in the second century to look through the northern arches into the interior of the fort. If the outer and inner gates were both open, this would have given an uninterrupted view along the east–west road, through the fort to the eastern gate, and the headquarters building would have been seen half-way through, on the left of the road. The gravel surface in front of the visitor is modern, but has been laid at the level where portions of the original gravel metalling of the Roman roadway were found. The sockets for outer gate-posts can be seen in the masonry, and on the left is the rectangular north guard-room, in which part of the guard on duty would have rested. The entrance into this from the passageway of the gate-house can be seen near the south-east corner of the room.

It must be understood that all this represents little more than half of the gate-house, and that to the south of the central piers was another passageway with inner and outer gates, and with a corresponding southern guard-room, a small portion of which was found but not preserved.

North of the northern guard-room extends a piece of the fort wall, built of Kentish ragstone like the piers and walls of the gate-house. The facing is of squared blocks laid in regular courses, but the core is of random lumps of ragstone set in mortar, making a hard rubble concrete. The only other material used here is to be seen in the projecting plinth of the west wall of the guard-room, which consists of blocks of sandstone, brought, like the ragstone, from the Maidstone district. In the upper surfaces of these are lewis-holes, used for attachment by means of an iron contrivance to a crane, when the great blocks were lifted.

Behind the fort wall is another ragstone wall, which is built hard against it—although a crevice is visible, showing that these are two distinct walls. The inner wall (to the east) was added as a thickening to the fort wall when the latter was incorporated in the city wall, in order to bring it to the standard thickness (8–9 feet) of the city wall elsewhere.

One other feature should be noted. There are the remains of a rather roughly built wall extending to the south from the outer pier of the gate, blocking the southern passageway. This originally continued across the northern entrance also, but was removed from here to uncover the socket of the gate-post. Its date is unknown, but its purpose was evidently to block the gateway. Since there is no record of a medieval gate here, this blocking presumably took place in Roman times or in the Dark Ages. It seems most likely that the final closing of the west gate of the fort coincided with the opening of a more conveniently placed city gate at Aldersgate. This appears to have been inserted in later Roman times *after* the building of the city wall.[1] The fort gate presumably remained in use as one of the city gates at least until this time, although it probably gave access only to minor roads.

On the south side of the new highway of London Wall, interesting traces of the Roman fort can be seen on the west side of Noble Street. The modern building-line follows that of the city wall, which coincides here with the west wall of the earlier fort. In the cellars of the bombed buildings the surviving portions of both the fort wall and the later Roman thickening have been excavated, but in places only the latter remains. Where the double wall with the fissure can be seen, it is the more westerly outer wall, which is farther from Noble Street, that is the original fort wall; while the inner is the thickening that was added when the city wall was built. The foundation of a small internal turret, built against the fort wall but not bonded into it, can be seen breaking the line of the inner thickening just over 50 yards south of the London Wall highway. (*Fig. 24,* **4**.) Small towers of this kind are characteristic features of Roman forts; each presumably contained a wooden stairway giving access both

[1] *RCL*, pp. 102 ff, 319.

to a rampart walk and to a higher vantage-point at the top of the tower.

About 30 yards farther south we come to the excavation that first revealed the existence of the fort and explained the curious shape of the city wall. Walking southward down Noble Street, immediately after passing Oat Lane on the left, the visitor will see the remains of a larger turret, not quite rectangular and set askew to the line of the city wall and of Noble Street. (*Fig. 24*, **5**.) It will be observed that the south-western wall of this structure is in fact a continuation of the fort wall, which here begins to curve to the east. It should be noted too that the inner thickening wall comes to an end at the north side of the turret. This is in fact the south-west corner of the fort, with a characteristic corner-turret within its curve. We are now at the apex of the Aldersgate re-entrant—the point where the city wall changes direction to a more westerly line. Here the later Roman city wall met the south-west corner of the fort, and a small portion of it at its junction with the fort wall can be seen between the latter and the modern wall to the west. The thickening that was added to the inside of the fort wall naturally comes to an end at the point where the fort wall ceases to form part of the city wall. A certain amount of modern reconstruction has been necessary to complete the ground-plan of these structures and make them intelligible, since they had been pierced by an office lift-shaft just at the meeting-point of the city and fort walls.

A portion of the V-shaped fort ditch, cut into the natural brick-earth, can still be seen to the south-west of the corner of the fort, where it is interrupted by the later Roman city wall. A Roman fort was invariably provided with a defensive ditch, and in this instance it seems also to have served for drainage. When it was blocked by the city wall it was replaced by the brick culvert that can be seen passing through the latter. This gave access to a gully overlying the fill of the ditch.

A bank of earth excavated from the ditch and foundation trench was originally piled up against the inner face of the wall, and traces of the lower part of this survive in places, as also do patches of the gravel metalling of the Roman roadway, which ran parallel to the wall.

A good idea of the size of the fort can be obtained by standing in Noble Street beside its south-west corner and looking northward to St Giles's Church, bearing in mind that the north wall of the fort lies immediately south of the church. This is a distance of more than 250 yards, and the total area enclosed by the walls is about 12 acres—less than a quarter of the size of the great fortresses that were the bases of legions at Caerleon and Chester, but larger than most auxiliary forts.

The London fort stands on ground that is a little higher than its immediate surroundings, but can hardly be described as a dominant position. It was sited well to the north and west of the main built-up areas of Londinium, in a district that had been very sparsely occupied. Its garrison was well placed to attack the left flank of an enemy approaching the city by land from the west, but apart from this the strategic value of the site is small. It could easily have been by-passed in any attack on the heart of the Roman city, which lay to the east of the Walbrook, separated from the fort by a region intersected by small streams, which was becoming increasingly marshy in the second century. The presence of a large body of troops in the neighbourhood would undoubtedly have given some protection to Londinium, and the effects of the rebellion in northern Britain at the beginning of Hadrian's reign may have been sufficiently

Fig. 29 *Reconstruction by Alan Sorrell, showing Londinium
at the time of the building of the city wall (about* AD 200);
*view from NW., with fort in foreground, and city wall as yet
built only to east of west wall of fort, although some work has
begun to the west of the fort. The Walbrook, basilica and forum,
and the governor's palace by the river can be seen in the distance*

far-reaching to demand new measures for the security of the capital.

There is also a possibility, which cannot be entirely ruled out,
that later troubles may have led to the building of the fort. London
was destroyed by fire for the second time between about AD 125
and 130, and it is generally thought that this was the result of an
accident, like the fire of 1666. There are, however, indications of
disturbance in Britain, unrecorded in history, about AD 130, and
this may have been the cause of the mysterious disappearance of the
Ninth Legion.[1] The fort was apparently unaffected by the fire, so it
is possible that it did not then exist, but was established as the
direct result of these troubles.

A somewhat earlier date for its construction is likely, however,
on the existing evidence, and its siting hardly suggests that the
defence of the city was the first consideration. Another explanation

[1] *Britannia*, pp. 137–40.

of its purpose has, therefore, been more generally accepted. London, as the capital of the province, would have had its troops for police and ceremonial duties, and as the administrative centre of a military government would also have had an army headquarters. (*See pp. 76–7.*) The fort may therefore have been built mainly as a barracks for these resident troops, perhaps with some accommodation for soldiers in transit, in a place that was conveniently near the town but sufficiently removed from the main concentration of the civilian population to ensure good discipline. The only difficulty about this interpretation is one of date. There is every indication that Londinium had achieved its full status as a provincial capital in Flavian times, whereas the fort can hardly be earlier than the reign of Trajan, and may well prove to be Hadrianic. There is no trace of an earlier fort on this site, and one wonders where these troops were accommodated in the thirty or forty years before the fort was built.

In view of the probability that police duties were one of the functions of the troops in the Cripplegate fort, it is an interesting coincidence that the headquarters of the 'Urban Cohort' of the modern City has been built on the site of one of their barracks. The visitor to the City Police headquarters can see some of the stones from this building, showing the tool-marks of the Roman masons, set in the inside wall on either side of the main entrance in Wood Street.

THE CITY WALL

Londinium was eventually enclosed on its landward sides by a great wall that was to mark the limits of the city for more than a thousand years, and to determine the line of many of its streets and property boundaries until the present day.

Like the fort wall, it was built of Kentish ragstone, faced on both sides with squared blocks laid in regular courses, and with a core of rubble concrete. The foundations, laid in a trench dug to a depth of several feet from the ancient surface, are of clay and flint or clay and ragstone. At the original ground-level the wall is about 9 feet thick, and on the outside is faced with a sandstone plinth; at a corresponding level in the inner face is a triple course of tiles, with a slight offset between the top and second tile. Just over 2 feet above this is a triple course of tiles, which runs right through the wall, and between its top and second tile is another offset on the inner face, reducing the thickness of the wall above its level to

117

about 8 feet. About 3 feet higher is a double course of tiles, also running through the wall, and again there is a slight reduction of thickness from the inner face. In places the wall has survived into recent times with a third similar bonding-course of tiles, 10 feet above the sandstone plinth, and traces of a fourth have been seen. We do not know the original height of the Roman wall, but it has been recorded as surviving to a height of 14½ feet above the plinth. It was partly rebuilt a number of times in the Middle Ages, and the portions that remain are almost wholly medieval above modern ground-level, with the original Roman wall surviving below it. A defensive ditch was dug outside the city wall, about 10 to 15 feet from its base, and the earth from this and from the foundation trench was piled against its inner face, to make a great bank, which probably rose almost to the height of the second bonding-course. At irregular intervals small rectangular towers were built, presumably containing wooden stairways giving access to a parapet above.

It has been known for a number of years that the city wall cannot have been built long before the end of the second century, for a worn coin of AD 183–4 was found in a deposit that had accumulated before the thickening was added to the wall of the fort. It seemed quite possible, however, that it was built considerably later, as was apparently the case at Canterbury, where a coin of about AD 270 antedated the earth-bank. The disturbances of the third quarter of the third century, when barbarians swept across Gaul and Saxon pirates raided Britain, seemed a likely background for the construction of massive defences. The provision of stone walls for the towns of Roman Britain was believed to be the outcome of a single imperial decision; and since some were being built soon after AD 270, it was assumed that the earliest were perhaps thirty years earlier, allowing that space of time for the completion of such a large programme. The wall of Verulamium, however, seems to have been in existence by about AD 240 at the latest, for a hoard of five coins, ending with one minted in 227–9, was concealed in the floor of one of its wall-towers.[1] In the last few years evidence has accumulated to suggest that the wall of Londinium was built earlier than this, probably within a decade of AD 200. A considerable amount of pottery from within and beneath the internal bank of the wall has been recovered on three different sites within the last seven years,[2] and in each case the result was the same as that obtained from a

---

[1] *Britannia*, pp. 252–3.
[2] Cooper's Row, Trinity Place and the Old Bailey.

section through the bank in the Tower of London in 1954.[1] The pottery antedating the bank ranged to the late second century, but did not include a scrap that could definitely be attributed to the third century. Further confirmation was obtained in 1965 from the eastern ditch of the fort which, on pottery evidence again, seems to have remained open until the late second century and then to have been covered with dumped clay. It seems unlikely that this would have been done before the eastern defences of the fort were made redundant by the city wall. The most convincing evidence, however, comes from an internal turret of the wall, found near the Old Bailey in 1966. After it had been built, refuse was dumped in it in layers—probably beneath the stairway. The earliest deposit contained pottery of about AD 200, and in the second were five coins, the latest being a silver denarius of AD 213–7 in almost mint condition; it had obviously not been in circulation very long before it was lost. In the same layer were found two double coin moulds that had been discarded by a forger. They contained impressions of silver denarii of Septimius Severus, Geta and Caracalla, which had also been in mint condition. These were datable to AD 201–10, 210–12 and 215 respectively. This layer was evidently deposited after the wall had been in existence for some little time, but its date can hardly be very much later than AD 225.

The evidence therefore points to an earlier period of disturbance for the building of London's wall, and the most likely historical context seems to be the unsettled years when Clodius Albinus, Governor of Britain, was making his bid for the Empire. To do so he was obliged to take most of the troops in Britain to fight on the Continent in AD 196, an eventuality that he must have foreseen at least two years earlier. The provision of defences for Romano-British towns would have been a wise precaution, and Professor Sheppard Frere has suggested that this was the occasion for the building of the earth-ramparts that were constructed in the late second century for such towns as Chichester, Dorchester-on-Thames and Silchester.[2] London, so far as we know, had no such earthworks, but it is inconceivable that no attempt would have been made to defend it. It seems likely that the capital was in fact given first priority, and that such resources of skilled labour as were available were concentrated there to build a masonry wall, while the defences of lesser towns were carried out by local levies, capable

[1] *Arch. Journ.*, CXII (1956), p. 23, footnote 3.
[2] *Britannia*, pp. 250–1.

only of constructing earthworks. Verulamium, where an earthwork was started but not completed, may have been high on the list, with walls only a little later than those of London, and belonging to the same earlier phase of town-fortification.

The magnitude of the Roman wall and its influence on the lay-out of the modern City of London can best be appreciated by following its line as closely as possible on foot—a walk of about $2\frac{1}{2}$ miles, allowing for necessary deviations. (The actual length of the wall is just over two miles.)

Starting at the eastern end, the first portion can be seen in the precincts of the Tower of London, where a piece of the bottom of the wall, about $10\frac{1}{2}$ feet long, has been preserved to the east of the White Tower, behind the ruins of the Wardrobe Tower, the lower

Fig. 30 *Roman city wall north of Tower Hill; view to south*

part of which was originally a bastion of the wall. (*Fig. 24*, **13**.) Most visitors will see this in the course of a general visit to the Tower, however, and a convenient starting-point for a tour of the city wall, involving no entrance fees, is the splendid piece of wall on the north side of Tower Hill, two minutes' walk from Tower Hill Station[1]. (*Fig. 24*, **12**.) (*Fig. 30*.) Here a sunken garden has been made where once there were cellars of buildings destroyed in the war. The grass surface is approximately at Roman ground-level, and above this rises the Roman wall with medieval rebuilding above it. At the northern end a particularly well-preserved piece of Roman wall can be seen, with the triple facing-course of tiles at the base and three tile bonding-courses above it. The original Roman facing of squared blocks of ragstone survives here to just above the uppermost bonding-course. At the southern end of the garden only the bottom of the wall survives, but projecting from it, immediately below Tower Hill, can be seen half of the base of one of the internal turrets, labelled 'site of Roman guard-house'—not the best possible description, although these small towers may, in addition to giving access to high look-out places and points of vantage, also have provided some shelter for sentries on duty.

Just to the north of this stretch of wall, in the remains of a bastion outside the wall, were found the fragments of the tombstone of Classicianus, the procurator, and a cast of the inscription from it has been set up in the garden. (*See pp. 69–71*.)

It is now necessary to leave the city wall and walk up Cooper's Row, which runs parallel to it at a distance of just over fifty yards. On the way, the visitor will pass the Toc H Club, where a piece of the Roman wall is preserved in the basement. The external face, with its sandstone plinth, can be seen here, but the Club is of course normally accessible only to members.

Just to the north of this, however, it is possible to return to the wall in the courtyard behind Midland House, 8–10 Cooper's Row, where one of the finest pieces has been preserved. (*Fig. 24*, **11**.) It survives to its medieval parapet, and in the upper part can be seen a window and four loop-holes for archers, as well as an indication of a stairway leading to the parapet walk. This part of the wall is early medieval, probably of about AD 1200. Below it the Roman wall can

---

[1] In Tower Hill Station itself, a small piece of the Roman wall can be seen in section, with a triple course of bonding-tiles at the top, in an opening high in the white tile wall south of platform 1 (westbound).

be seen, rising from the original ground-surface at the level of the basement car-park to a height of about thirteen feet—i.e. to just above the courtyard floor. It can be viewed from the courtyard by looking over the railing into the basement area. A considerable part of the facing of squared blocks of ragstone remains at the bottom of the inner face and at a higher level, but in between it has been removed, revealing the rubble core. It is possible to walk through an arched entrance made in recent times to the outside of the wall, at the bottom of which the sandstone plinth can be seen, corresponding in level with the triple tile-course on the inside.

After returning to Cooper's Row, and continuing northward beneath the railway, the visitor passes Crosswall (so called because it does—seventy yards to the east) and proceeds up Crutched Friars, which converges on the line of the wall. A substantial piece of the Roman structure, with its inner face practically intact to above the second bonding-course, has been preserved in the cellar of Roman Wall House. In Jewry Street to the north, the building-frontage on the east side follows the line exactly. A small piece of the wall is preserved in the basement of Sir John Cass College, and a larger piece survives in the cellar of the Three Tuns public house. The remains of the Roman wall that are on private property can, of course, be seen only by permission, as a special privilege.

From Jewry Street to Moorgate, modern streets—mostly of a secondary character—follow the line of the city wall very closely, and may be the successors of an ancient perimeter road along its inner side. The visitor who continues along them will see very little of archaeological interest, but will gain a new insight into the way in which the present shape of the City of London has been determined by events in the remote past. In several places he will be obliged to cross a busy thoroughfare, marking the position of one of the old gates of the city, where he is likely to be held up by cars and lorries as his predecessors were by horsemen and wagons.

First comes Aldgate, the gateway to Essex and Camulodunum— a most important route in the early Roman period, but probably much less so when the city wall was built. Excavations in 1967 revealed no trace of the Roman gate-house to the north of the building-frontage on the north side of the street, and it seems that its northern limit was represented by a foundation of flint and clay approximately parallel to the frontage, and just south of it. If so, Roman Aldgate must have been comparatively narrow, probably with only a single arch over a single carriageway.

Duke's Place to the north coincides with the line of the wall, the remains of which lie beneath the middle of the present road. Continuing in the same north-westerly direction are Bevis Marks and Camomile Street, also following the wall, which now lies on the north side of the modern streets, a little way behind the frontage. At its western end Camomile Street turns to a more westerly direction as it approaches Bishopsgate, reflecting a curve in the wall at this point. Parallel with these streets to the north is Houndsditch, named after the great ditch that was dug in the thirteenth century. The Roman ditch was very much smaller (10–16 feet wide) and V-shaped in section. In many places it lay considerably nearer the wall, and so escaped being totally destroyed by the later city ditch.

Bishopsgate was the Roman gate that led to Ermine Street and the north, but practically nothing is known of its shape or structure. A mass of ragstone rubble masonry on a foundation of clay with flints, found in 1905 near the north angle of Wormwood Street, probably formed part of the gate-house. There was also of course a medieval gate, and it is interesting to note that here, as at Aldgate and Aldersgate, is a church dedicated to St Botolph, who evidently took a special interest either in travellers or in the protection of cities.

West of Bishopsgate, Wormwood Street and London Wall follow the line of the city wall, and part of the medieval wall, very much restored, can be seen on the north side of the churchyard, west of All Hallows Church. The outer face of the Roman wall below this was uncovered in 1905, and beneath the plinth was found a brick culvert, through which had passed the waters of the eastern branch of the Walbrook. To the east, the base of the Roman wall underlies the north wall of the church, and the projecting vestry is built on one of the bastions, part of which can be seen from the office buildings to the north. Continuing westward, the line of the city wall runs beneath the northern part of the wider roadway of London Wall, and Moorgate is reached. This is the site of a late medieval gate, which was built on the site of an earlier medieval postern. As far as know, there was no Roman gate here—nor any reason for one, as no Roman road seems to have left the city at this point.

Until recently the street of London Wall followed the line of the city wall to the west of Moorgate—so closely that it was possible to see a distinct kink in the modern street at the point where a slight change in the direction of the wall marked its junction with the north-east corner of the earlier fort. The old street, however, has been replaced by the new double highway that cuts across the north-west corner of the old city. This is still called London Wall, but the name is misleading, as it no longer follows the wall. Near its eastern end the new highway intersects the line, and a good piece of the Roman wall has been preserved in the underground car-park beneath it. It survives from the triple facing-course of tiles at the base, which was near the ancient ground-level, to above the second bonding-course. Unfortunately it can only be seen by users of the car-park, and pedestrian visitors are not admitted.

It is better to go up to the new upper-level walk for the first view of the next piece of wall, which is perhaps the most interesting of all, since it demonstrates almost the entire history of the city's defences. (*Fig. 31.*) This is the north wall of St Alphage's churchyard, which survives as a small green oasis below the breezy promenade deck of the High Walk. (*Fig. 24,* **6**.) It can easily be found with the help of a

Fig. 31 *Roman and medieval city wall, St Alphage churchyard, London Wall, showing double Roman wall at base, the outer (right) being the remains of the original fort wall, and the inner (left) the thickening added when the city wall was built. View to W*

near-by landmark on the south side of the latter—the ruin of the fourteenth-century church-tower that originally belonged to the Priory of Elsing Spital.[1] A visit to this impressive piece of the city wall can conveniently be combined with one to Guildhall Museum, in the temporary quarters that it occupies on the Bassishaw High Walk (south of the highway) until the Museum of London is built.

The best view of the wall is from the north-east, whence it will be seen that the base is in fact a double wall, containing no trace of the tile-courses that are so characteristic of the lower (Roman) part of the city wall elsewhere. This is because we have now reached the Roman fort, and the outer wall at the base is what remains of its north wall. The inner wall, separated from the outer by a distinct fissure, is the thickening that was added to the north wall of the fort when it was incorporated with the city wall—in exactly the same way as was done with the west wall, which has already been described. (See pp. 113–14.) It will be noted, however, that the outer wall is comparatively thin, and lacks its original facing. It is clear that the outer side was reduced and refaced with masonry at some unknown but early period. Above this is medieval rebuilding, in which at least three different styles can be distinguished. These can best be seen by going down into the garden on the north side of the wall. One portion is faced with ashlar in which there are courses of knapped flint and tiles; it can be closely paralleled in the mid-fourteenth-century additions to St Katharine's Chapel at Westminster Abbey, and must be of about the same date. Finally there are the brickwork battlements, which are attributed to Sir Ralph Jocelyn, the Lord Mayor who repaired the wall in 1476. The diaper pattern of red and black bricks can just be distinguished from the churchyard side, although the bricks now appear almost uniformly black.

To the west of this piece of wall is the site of Cripplegate, at the northern end of Wood Street—the one city gate that never opened on to a major road, and is marked only by minor streets today. (See p. 111.) The line of the wall to the west was followed by the south wall of St Giles's churchyard, and a portion of it remains. This will eventually be made accessible, and it will be possible to see, projecting from its north side, pieces of the walls of the newly discovered thirteenth-century bastion.

[1] The priory church was given to the parish of St Alphage after the Dissolution of the Monasteries, and replaced the old parish church. From this time, until its destruction in the Second World War, the parish church stood on the opposite side of the street to its churchyard.

South-west of St Giles's Church the wall changes direction, turning sharply through 90° towards the south. At this point which, as we have already seen, was the north-west corner of the Roman fort that determined the shape of the later city wall, stands the medieval corner-bastion (Bastion 12). Farther south, the curved western end of a bombed site, once occupied by the courtroom of Barber-Surgeons' Hall, indicates the position of another bastion (13), and a third medieval bastion (14), with a blocked window opening and arrow-slits, still stands just north of the new highway of London Wall.

The bastions of London are of two kinds: a group with solid cores, which (with one possible exception) are confined to the eastern part of the city; and a group that are hollow to their bases, found in the western part of the city, but occurring also at All Hallows Church on the north side, and in the Tower of London (Wardrobe Tower) in the east. The only bastions of which visible portions survive belong to this second group.

Until recently it was thought that all the bastions were late Roman in origin, although they had evidently been rebuilt in medieval times. This was a reasonable assumption, as projecting towers of this kind were characteristic of the fortifications of the late third and fourth centuries, their purpose being to provide platforms for *ballistae*, the Roman spring-guns, which could then cover the approaches up to the foot of the wall. The discovery in 1948 of a pendant, attributed to the eighth or ninth century, on the original floor of Bastion 14, threw considerable doubt on the Roman origin of the western group of hollow bastions, and it was thought that they might have been built by the orders of King Alfred, when he refortified the city in 883. The evidence was not conclusive, however, as it seemed possible that the pendant might be intrusive. The problem was convincingly solved, however, when a hitherto unknown bastion (11A), between Cripplegate and the corner-bastion, was found and excavated in 1966. Details of its construction indicated that it was built at the same time as its neighbours to the west, and this time the dating evidence was clear. A deposit of refuse, which had accumulated before the bastion was built, contained medieval pottery of a kind that is attributed to the thirteenth century.[1] It seems, therefore, that the bastions in this area—and probably all the other hollow bastions—are neither late Roman nor Anglo-

[1] *JRS*, LVII (1967), p. 191.

Saxon, but medieval in origin. The hollow bastion at All Hallows Church (Bastion 11) was believed to be Roman, because its footings, which overlay the Roman ditch, had apparently been laid while the ditch was still open.[1] Recent excavations at Aldgate, however, have shown that an early medieval ditch, antedating the great medieval ditch called Houndsditch, was cut almost on the line of the Roman ditch, and it now seems possible that it was this that remained open when the bastion was built.

If the hollow bastions are of medieval origin, what of the solid bastions in the wall between Bishopsgate and Tower Hill? These contained a great deal of Roman material—stone from Roman buildings and especially from Roman monuments in the cemeteries outside the wall, used as building material to form their cores. They were evidently built while these structures were still standing—or were, at any rate, clearly visible above ground. Their Roman origin is still generally accepted, partly for this reason, but mainly because it would be extraordinary if London were omitted when bastions were added to the walls of most towns of Roman Britain after the middle of the fourth century—probably by Count Theodosius after the barbarian invasions of 367.[2] It has, however, been recalled that a piece of green-glazed pottery is said to have been found beneath the masonry near the centre of the Camomile Street Bastion,[3] and such ware was very common in the Middle Ages, and very rare in Roman Britain, where it normally only occurs in early contexts. The date of the solid bastions therefore remains an open question, but it must not be forgotten that Fitzstephen, writing in 1174, said that the wall of London had towers at intervals on the north side. If these were not bastions, what were they? Moreover, he implies that they were of considerable antiquity in his day by referring to a tradition (probably incorrect[4]) that there was formerly a similar wall with towers on the south side of the city, but that with the passage of time, this had been destroyed by the ebb and flow of the Thames.[5] It seems therefore that some bastions at least were already old when the thirteenth-century bastions were built west of Cripplegate.

Continuing on the line of the wall south of Bastion 14, we come

---

[1] *Arch.*, LXIII (1912), p. 274.
[2] *Britannia*, p. 256.
[3] J. E. Price: *On a Bastion of London Wall*, 1880, p. 26.
[4] See pp. 131–2.
[5] William Fitzstephen: *Descriptio Nobilissimae Civitatis Londiniae*. (Quoted in Stow's *Survey of London*, Kingsford edition, II, p. 220).

to the remains of the fort, which have already been described (*pp. 112–15*)—the west gate, which probably continued in use for a while as a city gate, and the west wall with its thickening, which formed the Roman city wall here. Above it, on the south side of the modern highway, a portion of the core of the medieval wall can be seen standing well above the present ground-level. For the most part, however, the line to the west of Noble Street is represented only by the double Roman wall at basement-level and by a nineteenth-century brick wall above it.

West of the south-west corner of the fort can be seen the base of the city wall that adjoined it, pierced with a brick culvert, as previously described (*p. 115*). From this position the line of the wall continued to the south-west, and it is followed by the south wall of the modern building (Alder House) to the north of the Church of St Anne and St Agnes. Here, as elsewhere, the ancient wall, which no longer survives above ground, has determined the boundary of the site, and hence the shape of the building upon it. The angle between this line of wall and the north–south line, which incorporated the west wall of the fort, was formerly occupied by a hollow bastion (Bastion 15). Its northern end can be seen adjoining the outside of the fort wall to the north of the corner turret, but only a very small piece remains, as it is cut by the modern brick wall. The way in which this bastion was constructed, with its base sloping up to the face of the city wall, is exactly the same as was found in Bastion 14 and the recently discovered thirteenth-century bastion (11A). There seems no doubt that it was built at the same time—when the base of the wall against which it was built was already more than a thousand years old.

To reach the line of the city wall again, it is necessary to continue to the southern end of Noble Street, turning right at Gresham Street and right again at Aldersgate Street. The line is reached opposite the entrance of Alder House, and here stood Roman Aldersgate, which had a double gateway with bastion-like towers projecting on the outside. It was slightly askew to the line of the wall, with its two central piers beneath the pavement on the east side of the street, so that most of the eastern half was beneath Alder House. A portion of the masonry of the projecting western tower was found beneath the middle of Aldersgate Street during tunnelling in 1939, when the central piers were also observed. The gate had apparently been inserted after the building of the wall, or at least after its foundations had been laid, as the northern pier cut through its flint and clay footings.[1]

The line of the wall can be traced a little farther by crossing to the west side of Aldersgate Street and entering St Botolph's Church-yard, now known as Postman's Park. A stretch of the Roman wall is actually preserved here, in the basement area of the G.P.O. Headquarters building, but it can only be seen from inside and is not accessible to the public. It forms the southern boundary of the churchyard, however, so that its line can be followed although no wall is visible. The projecting portion of the G.P.O. building at the western end of Postman's Park is actually on the site of one of the bastions. West of King Edward Street the wall continues on the same line, but is no longer exactly marked by any modern topographi-cal feature. The northern face of the G.P.O. building here is set at a slight angle to it, so that the line from east to west passes from just outside the building to within it.

Inside the G.P.O. yard east of Giltspur Street, the wall turns to the south, and, as might be expected, the rounded corner was protected with a bastion—almost certainly medieval. A considerable part of this, with a portion of the Roman wall adjoining it to the east, has been preserved below ground and can be visited, Monday to Friday only, by arrangement with the Postmaster[2] (*Fig. 24*, **1**).

Forty yards to the south we come to the busy highway of Newgate Street, the main route from the city to the west and north-west since Roman times. We know much more about the Roman gate here than any of the others. In plan it was very much like the west gate of the fort, but was on a much larger scale. Its square towers were four times the size of those of the fort gate, and its double carriage-way was nearly twelve yards wide. The northern guard-room lay for the most part beneath 121 and 122 Newgate Street, with its southern edge approximately on the kerb-line; the southern, as the result of road-widening to the south, lay mostly beneath the pavement and roadway, with only its southern edge beneath the building-line.

The city wall to the south runs almost parallel to the street of Old Bailey, and about thirty yards to the east of it. A piece of the foundation and lower part of the Roman wall has been preserved beneath the new extension to the Central Criminal Court, north of Warwick Square, and will eventually be accessible to the public by arrangement, on application to the Keeper of the Court. (*Fig. 24*, **2**). It was unfortunately impracticable to preserve also the very

[1] *RCL*, p. 319 (**G8**).
[2] Write to the Postmaster, G.P.O., St Martin's-le-Grand, or telephone 01–432 3176.

Fig. 32 *Base of city wall with internal turret as excavated,
site of Old Bailey extension. View from above to S.*

interesting internal turret that adjoined it a little farther south.
(*See p. 119.*) (*Fig. 32.*)

It is popularly believed that the stone wall on the west side of
Amen Court is part of the city wall, but during excavations in
1907–8 the Roman wall was found seven feet to the west of it. It
has been suggested that the Amen Court wall was in fact the
boundary wall of the precinct of St Paul's. At one point a tower,
apparently of the sixteenth century, had been inserted between the
two walls, partly cut into the thickness of the city wall; and in another
place a thick chalk wall, evidently medieval, had been built on the
inside of the Roman wall.[1] It is clear that modifications in the city
defences took place in this area in post-Roman times, and the
relationship of the Amen Court wall to these is as yet unknown. It is
certain, however, that it stands well inside the Roman line.

[1] Arch., LXIII, pp. 295–304.

The line of the wall meets Ludgate Hill on the east side of *Ye Olde London* public house, and here stood Ludgate, almost certainly a Roman gate, but one of which we know nothing. We know very little more about the Roman city wall itself south of Ludgate Hill. The surrounding land was given to the Dominican Friars in the late thirteenth century, and they were allowed to pull it down, the city wall subsequently being reconstructed to enclose the new priory. It was extended westward along the north side of the modern Pilgrim Street and then southward along the east side of the Fleet River. We have no certain archaeological record of any discovery of the older wall, and a considerable part of it had probably been obliterated at an even earlier date when two Norman strongholds, Baynard's Castle and the Tower of Mountfiquit, were built in this area. Two modern alleys, however, lie immediately opposite the line of the wall north of Ludgate, and seem to continue its line, with a very slight deflection such as normally occurs on the opposite side of a gate. These are Cobbs Court and Church Entry, north and south of Carter Lane. Church Entry marks the position of the central tower between the nave and choir of the priory church of Blackfriars and, to the south, the east side of its cloister.[1] It seems likely that the Dominicans' plan was influenced by existing topographical features, and the old city wall would have been an obvious dividing line between the two parts of the priory. Some support for this view is given by vague records of discoveries of a massive wall in the mid-nineteenth century. Roach Smith described such a wall on the site of the *Times* office to the south, and said that it was of three distinct constructions: the Roman city wall; a Norman or early medieval reconstruction; and above, the remains of a passage or window belonging to the Blackfriars Priory.[2]

Massive walls have been recorded from time to time near the Roman water-front under Upper and Lower Thames Street, but they do not seem to have formed part of a continuous defensive wall. A long stretch of wall extending eastward from Lambeth Hill was observed by Roach Smith when excavations were being made for the sewer in the middle of Upper Thames Street; this, however, did not continue west of Lambeth Hill, but 'formed an angle'.[3] In fact, it seems to have made a right-angle, turning to the north up the west side of Lambeth Hill. Other very thick walls were seen in this

[1] See *Arch.*, LXIII, Pl. XI.
[2] *JBAA*, 1st. ser., V, p. 155.
[3] *IRL*, pp. 18–19.

area during excavations for the Salvation Army International Headquarters in 1961, and it seems that a large Roman structure was built here on the hillside, which was artificially terraced.[1] The riverside wall may have formed part of this, or may have been a quayside associated with it. Other portions of riverside walls found farther east can likewise best be explained as embankments or quays, for they were not uniform in construction and do not seem to have been continuous. It must be assumed that there was some kind of riverside fortification at each end of the city wall, and there may well have been other defences on the water-front, but there is no evidence for a continuous defensive wall along the river-bank, in any way comparable with that on the landward side.

[1] *LAMAS Trans.*, XXI, pt. 3 (1967), pp. 149–54.

CHAPTER EIGHT

Beyond the City Limits

Immediately outside the boundaries of the Roman city was the city of the dead. It was the custom, sanctioned by law, that burials should be outside the inhabited area, and for convenience they were usually placed near the roads leading out of town. As Londinium grew, however, the city of the living encroached on that of the dead, so that some of the earlier burial-grounds were eventually, wholly or in part, enclosed by the city wall.

One cemetery lay to the east, south of Aldgate High Street, in the neighbourhood of the Minories and Goodman Fields, and here the ashes of Classicianus, the procurator, were presumably laid, beneath the impressive memorial that was later to be used as building material in a neighbouring bastion. (*See pp. 69–71.*) A tomb-stone of a married legionary of the Sixth Legion found in Goodman Fields, and now in the London Museum, is of much later date, since serving soldiers were not allowed to marry before the end of the second century.[1] Even later is a decorated sarcophagus from the Minories in the British Museum: it is likely to have been made at least 250 years after the death of Classicianus, so that this burial-ground evidently continued in use for most of the Roman period. Painted wall-plaster has been found near burials in the Minories, and it seems likely that some of the tombs were fairly elaborate though flimsy structures.

Another cemetery lay to the north, extending from the east side of Bishopsgate to the west of Finsbury Pavement, and here no doubt stood the monument to the legionary soldier whose stone effigy, now in Guildhall Museum, was found in the Camomile Street

[1] *RIB*, 11.

K

Fig. 33 *Limestone group originally from monument in cemetery, showing lion killing deer, found re-used as building material in bastion of city wall, Camomile Street*

bastion. A sculptured group representing a lion killing a deer, found in the same bastion, is also in the Museum. (*Fig. 33.*) This was a popular subject for funerary sculpture, and perhaps conceals some religious idea that we do not fully understand, behind the obvious symbolism of the cruelty of death. It would no doubt originally have stood on a pedestal over a grave in the northern cemetery. The scant respect with which these monuments were used by the builders of the bastions may be due to an emergency rather than to deliberate desecration of the old pagan tombs. A number of cinerary urns and other complete pots from grave groups in Bishopsgate, Liverpool Street and Moorfields are in Guildhall Museum.

The western cemetery was more extensive, and really consisted of several distinct burial-grounds. The nearest and earliest was in the neighbourhood of St Martin's-le-Grand, continuing southward to St Paul's Cathedral, where Roman burials were found by Wren's workmen. This shows that the Roman city did not originally extend beyond the western ends of Cheapside and Cannon Street. Other cremation burials and one inhumation have been found within the city wall south of Newgate, and these presumably antedate the wall. A magnificent urn of porphyry and a lead canister with a relief of Sol driving his chariot, both found here, can be seen in the British Museum. (*Fig. 34*, **a** and **b**.)

(a)   (b)

Fig. 34 (a) *Lead canister with relief representing Sol in his chariot and* (b) *porphyry urn that both contained cremations, found in Warwick Square*

Beyond the wall there was a considerable cemetery in the Smithfield area and in the neighbourhood of Holborn Viaduct; while a scatter of burials also continued farther west on both sides of the Roman road through Holborn. (*See p. 46.*)

Farther south, no actual burials have been recorded between St Paul's Cathedral and the River Fleet, but several important funerary monuments were found in or near Ludgate Hill, and it seems likely that they originally stood in the same neighbourhood. They include the heavy stone pedestal dedicated to Claudia Martina, at present in Guildhall Crypt (*p. 74*), and the seven-foot gravestone of Vivius Marcianus, a centurion of the Second Legion Augusta, which was found during the rebuilding of St Martin's Church, Ludgate, in 1669, and is now in the Ashmolean Museum at Oxford. It seems unlikely that either would have been moved far from the grave on which it stood.

West of the Fleet, cremation burials have been found near the southern end of Shoe Lane, and immediately opposite, on the southern side of Fleet Street, is the Christian cemetery of St Bride's, where Professor Grimes found very early burials. It could not be ascertained whether any of these were late Roman, but it has been suggested that there is a strong probability of some link between this graveyard and the Roman cemetery, and that continuity of use may have attracted an early church with Celtic dedication to this spot.[1]

[1] Professor W. F. Grimes: 'Excavations in the City of London', in R. L. S. Bruce-Mitford (ed.): *Recent Archaeological Excavations in Britain*, 1956, p. 116.

This raises a very interesting question, to which a final answer cannot be given owing to lack of evidence. The visitor, on application to the verger, can descend beneath the nave of the present building to see the remains of an early church, dating from about the time of the Norman Conquest, the eastern apse of which had replaced an earlier east end of uncertain character. To the east of this a small portion of a Roman pavement of coarse red tesserae has also been preserved. It is just visible reflected in the left-hand (northern) mirror above the eastern end of the early church, while detached tesserae and painted wall-plaster from the building are shown in a case in the crypt. Unfortunately there was no archaeological evidence of the nature of the structure, and possibilities can only be suggested by analogy with what has been found elsewhere.

The Roman building stood outside the south-east corner of a large ditched enclosure, also of unknown purpose, the angle of which was found under the north-west part of the church.[1] Its ditch had been filled up by natural processes quite early in the Roman period. There was no evidence of date for the building with the tessellated floor, and it is just possible that it was associated with the enclosure and was built before the cemetery existed. The cremations found in Shoe Lane, however, seem to range from a very early date at least to the late third century, so that it is more likely that the building co-existed with the cemetery. If so, it is doubtful whether it can have been an ordinary dwelling-place, since the living usually avoided close proximity with the dead.

A possible parallel was found a few years ago to the south-east of Verulamium. Here, a small apsidal building with a floor in red tesserae was excavated near a Roman cemetery that was still in use in Christian times. Near by was found a fragment of the drapery of a bronze statue, believed to be of the fourth century, which may be connected with it.[2] It seems likely that it was a shrine of some sort, and its association with the cemetery suggests that it is more likely to have been Christian than pagan, since the cult of the blessed dead was important to the early Christians. It is possible that the Roman building in Fleet Street was something of the same kind and, if so, its position on a site later occupied by the sanctuary of a church may be significant. Recent excavations in the ruined church of Stone, near Faversham, have shown that a small Roman building was there incorporated in the chancel of the medieval church. In

[1] *JRS*, XLIV (1954), p. 98.
[2] Details of this discovery were kindly supplied by Dr Ilid Anthony in advance of its publication.

this case, also, the building was associated with burials, some pagan, and it is suggested that it was originally a temple or mausoleum.[1] Buildings in Romano-British cemeteries were evidently sometimes deliberately selected as sites for English churches, and there is no reason why this should not have occurred in London; but in the absence of evidence to bridge the chronological gap between the Roman building under St Bride's and the Anglo-Norman church, it cannot be assumed that there was any continuity of the cult.

A piece of mosaic pavement, with a geometric pattern in black, red and white, was found in the seventeenth century near St Andrew's Church, Holborn, and a Roman burial in an oak box with a number of pots, apparently a cremation, was dug up in the roadway opposite this church when the sewer was laid in 1833. Other burials have been found not very far away.[2] It is curious that here also there seems to be an association between Roman graves, a Roman building just beyond the River Fleet, and an English church of early origin. A reference is made in King Edgar's Westminster Charter of 959 to 'the old wooden church of St Andrew', standing beside the 'wide army street' (the Roman road from Newgate), and it is a reasonable assumption that this was on or very near the site of the later church.[3] It does not of course necessarily follow that the Roman pavement 'near' the seventeenth-century church was on the site of the ancient church or even in very close proximity to it. Nevertheless, the coincidence is sufficiently remarkable, in view of the fact that these two tessellated pavements near both ends of Shoe Lane, each lying immediately west of the Fleet valley and south of a Roman highway, are the only *certain* indications of Roman buildings that have been recorded in three hundred years between the west wall of the city and Westminster. We would very much like to know what they were.

A very doubtful structure, found on the site of a medieval church, was the arch discovered when the present church of St Martin-in-the-Fields was built in 1722. Stukeley described it as being built of Roman brick with a floor of strong cement, and with several ducts side by side running along its wall. If this was in fact Roman, it seems likely to have been a flue-channel for heating. There is no reason to suppose that it was connected with any religious or

---

[1] *The Times*, 7 September 1967.
[2] *RCHM : RL*, p. 147.
[3] Margaret Gelling: 'The Boundaries of the Westminster Charters', in *LAMAS Trans.*, N.S., XI (1953), pp. 101–3.

funerary structure; although a burial with a glass vessel in a stone coffin was found when the foundations of the portico were dug.[1]

An undoubted Roman building seems to have stood on the site of Westminster Abbey, where, in the nineteenth century, concrete flooring and roof-tiles were found in the cloister and in digging the foundations of Canons' houses in the Abbey garden, and what appeared to be the remains of the *pilae* of a hypocaust were actually found under the nave of the Abbey church.[2] This building was evidently domestic; and one of its inhabitants was probably the Valerius Amandinus whose sarcophagus, found re-used for a later burial on the north side of the church, can now be seen in the entrance to the Chapter House. The Roman burial in this instance was an appendage of an outlying settlement, and does not indicate the presence of a cemetery for general use. The environment of the building was therefore very different from that of the two structures just outside Londinium. Nevertheless, this also is associated with the site of an English church, which may have been in existence as early as the seventh century. It is quite possible, therefore, that the ruins of isolated Roman buildings attracted the founders of early English churches, regardless of their nature. They may still have provided some shelter, and were probably a useful source of building material. Was it perhaps also considered that the most certain way to exorcise the ghosts on useful sites was to sanctify the ruins in this way? It can hardly be coincidence that the only three substantial Roman buildings in Central London, west of Londinium, for which we have evidence—and the possible fourth—should all be closely associated with later churches. (Another example, a little farther out, is the old parish church of St Andrew, Kingsbury, which is said to have been surrounded by an ancient earthwork as recently as the eighteenth century, and which has Roman flue-tiles, presumably from a building on the site, incorporated in the chancel walls.[3])

At this point the reader may be asking: 'What about the Roman bath in the Strand?', and the vexed question of this mysterious structure must now be discussed. Its actual position is in Strand Lane, south of the Strand, and it can be visited between 10 a.m. and 12.30 p.m. on weekdays (admission 1/-). Like the two Thames Street bath-houses it makes use of springs emerging from the slope above the river, and these still supply it. It is built of brick, and the

[1] *RCHM: RL*, p. 147.
[2] Ibid., p. 148.
[3] *RCHM: Middlesex*, 1937, p. 89; *JBAA* (N.S.) XXXV, pp. 282–4.

marble facing which has now been removed was comparatively modern. The dimensions are $15\frac{1}{2}$ feet long by $6\frac{3}{4}$ feet wide, and the western end is rounded. The earliest reference to it is in 1784, and it probably came to light when a cottage on the site was burnt down in 1774. It is quite certain, therefore, that it is earlier than the eighteenth century, but its depth, at only $4\frac{1}{2}$ feet below the present ground-level, hardly suggests that it is very ancient. The brickwork has a superficial resemblance to Roman work, for the bricks are only $1\frac{3}{4}$ inches thick, about the usual thickness of Roman tiles. The face of the wall, where only the edges can be seen, therefore looks remarkably Roman. The other dimensions, however, are about 9 inches by 5 inches, and conform approximately with the proportions of the bricks used in the last four or five hundred years—bricks designed for handling with one hand, and much smaller than the normal tile-like Roman bricks, which are about 16 by 10 inches. It has been suggested that the bath, with another that lay farther south, was originally a reservoir used for domestic purposes in the sixteenth or seventeenth century. During this period, the site was occupied by a building of unknown use in the grounds of Arundel House, the great town mansion of the Earls of Arundel, where a large supply of water would have been required. Nevertheless, the rounded end certainly makes the structure look more like a bath than a reservoir.

One thing seems reasonably certain, regardless of the question of age: it did not belong to a Roman public bath-house, which required a large clientele. Where would the customers have come from? No Roman Londoner, needing the relaxation and frivolity of the baths, would have walked more than half a mile beyond the city gate, crossing the Fleet River and passing through a cemetery to get there. Nor can we imagine the long-distance traveller stopping there to refresh himself and to remove the grime of the journey before entering Londinium; for this was a road that linked the city with neighbouring riverside settlements like the one at Westminster, and it would not have been much used by travellers from distant towns. All coming from Verulamium and probably most from Silchester would have approached London by the main road that led to Newgate. If it were of Roman date, the Strand Lane bath could only have belonged to a luxurious private villa, and some other evidence for a large building of this kind would surely have been observed in the neighbourhood.

The unusual character of the bricks suggests an attempt to

imitate Roman brickwork in more recent times, and it is possible that this gives us a clue to the person who was responsible for it. One of the owners of the site was Thomas Howard, second Earl of Arundel and Surrey, who died in 1646. He travelled in Italy, and was the first collector of classical antiquities in this country. Is it not possible that he had a 'Roman bath' or perhaps a *nymphaeum* (an ornamental pool dedicated to the water nymphs), with other appropriate architectural features, built in the grounds of his London house as a suitable setting for some of his antique sculptures?[1] If so, the bath would be no less interesting as a forerunner of the numerous 'follies' of the next century.

It is clear that there was no suburban development beyond the walls of Londinium, and the only true suburb was in Southwark, where a cluster of dwellings grew up at an early date, mainly to the west of the bridge, and gradually spread in the second century in a ribbon development for a few hundred yards along Stane Street. The lateral growth of the settlement was hindered by the low-lying character of the ground to the east and west, which, in spite of drainage, became increasingly marshy in later Roman times. Development to the east was particularly limited owing to the presence of a large water-channel.

We know very little about the character of the Roman suburb, and the suggestion has been made that it had something of the raffishness for which Southwark was notorious in later ages. Here, it has been conjectured, we might expect to find traces of the missing places of entertainment of Londinium—its amphitheatre and theatre—probably built mainly of wood. As yet there is no evidence to support this view, for the single trident, believed to be gladiatorial, which was found in Stoney Street and is now in

Fig. 35 *Iron trident, possibly of a gladiator, from Stoney Street*

[1] I am indebted to Mr F. J. Collins for this suggestion. For details of the history of the bath, see the LCC pamphlet: *The 'Roman' Bath, Strand Lane*, 1964.

140

Guildhall Museum, is a portable object that might have been dropped anywhere. (*Fig. 35.*) From its condition, it is likely that it was recovered from a riverside deposit at the northern end of the street, and would therefore belong to the large series of objects that were lost in the Thames. In this context its apparent association with a pre-Roman iron dagger and pottery of the first century would mean very little.[1] Similarly, the wine-jug in the London Museum, inscribed LONDINI AD FANUM ISIDIS ('London, at the Shrine of Isis'), although found in Tooley Street, Southwark, does not necessarily indicate that the temple of the Egyptian goddess actually stood here. If it did, it would consort well with the rather disreputable character that has been attributed to the suburb, for Isis was especially honoured by prostitutes, and her temples were frequented by young men in search of amorous adventures.[2] The jug, which is probably of the later first century, may have come from a tavern near the temple. (*See fig. 53, p. 181.*)

It is possible that a fairly large building found beneath King's Head Yard, on the east side of Borough High Street, south of St Thomas Street, was an inn—the Roman precursor of a succession of medieval and later inns on the same site.[3] We have no clue at all, however, to the nature of the most substantial Roman building recorded in Southwark. This stood on the south side of Southwark Cathedral, where tessellated floors have been found, and it probably also extended on to the site of the church itself, since stone foundations, believed to be Roman, were found under the choir. A small piece of the tessellated pavement has been set into the Cathedral floor at the entrance to the south chancel aisle.

Southwark had its own burial-grounds outside the suburb in the neighbourhood of the roads to Sussex and Kent. There are rather vague references to the discovery of cinerary urns, skeletons and grave-furniture near Borough High Street, and definite records of both cremations and the later inhumations near the supposed line of Watling Street where it approaches Stane Street. If, as is believed, this corresponds approximately with Old Kent Road and Tabard Street (*p. 61*), the cemetery lies mainly on its south-western side, for groups of burials have been found in Deverell Street and Trinity Street.

Outside Londinium and its southern suburb, the Romano-

[1] *JBAA*, 1st. ser., XXIV (1868), pp. 309–12.
[2] F. Cumont: *Oriental Religions in Roman Paganism*, Dover edition, 1956, pp. 90–1.
[3] K. M. Kenyon: *Excavations in Southwark*, 1959, p. 21.

British communities in Greater London were small and scattered. Much of the food supply of the Roman city mut have come from the land now covered by the sprawl of modern London; and the majority of these settlements were probably isolated farmsteads. Evidence of occupation has been found in Downing Street, Putney[1] and Clapham Common (South Side), and late Roman burials have been found in Battersea Park; but none of these sites have yet produced any trace of substantial Roman buildings, comparable with that at Westminster Abbey, where the presence of a hypocaust suggests comfortable living, and a degree of prosperity is indicated by the inscribed sarcophagus. The existence of another well-to-do household, presumably a farm, in the Hackney Marshes in late Roman times, is similarly demonstrated by the fine marble sarcophagus from Lower Clapton, exhibited in the crypt of Guildhall. (*See p. 53.*) This was certainly not used for the burial of a peasant-woman or farm-servant.

It is remarkable, however, that nowhere within a large radius of the Roman city is there any indication of a really luxurious villa, of the kind that was fairly common in the countryside, especially in the fourth century. Such villas usually had fine mosaic pavements, which seldom escape notice, even in the course of builders' excavations. The fact that none have been observed during the building of London beyond the City and Southwark suggests that villas of this class did not exist in the neighbourhood. The nearest fine mosaic that has so far been recorded is one found in the eighteenth century in Wanstead Park, almost six miles from Londinium.[2]

There was an important building considerably nearer than this in Greenwich Park, where a tiny piece of floor of coarse red tesserae has been preserved, and can be seen within a small enclosure among trees in the northern part of the Park. It is about one hundred yards from the east wall, half-way between the Vanbrugh and Maze Hill Gates. Very little is known about this building, of which only a small piece of ragstone wall and three patches of flooring have been found—not enough to give any indication of its plan. Hypocaust bricks, painted wall-plaster, cubes from a mosaic, window glass and fragments of columns have been found, as well as about three hundred coins, ranging from Claudius to Honorius, but mostly

---

[1] Excavations by the Wandsworth Historical Society, in the neighbourhood of the eastern end of Lower Richmond Road, have revealed indeterminate structures of modest character, and Roman cremations of the 1st and 2nd centuries. There are also coin finds, ranging from the 1st to the later 4th century.

[2] *VCH Essex*, III, p. 198; *Arch.*, I (1779), p. 73.

Constantinian. The most important finds, however, were a piece of a sculptured figure and small fragments of several different inscriptions, one of sandstone and the rest of white marble.[1] They are all unfortunately too incomplete to be reconstructed, or even to give any definite idea of their subject-matter. There is a hint of a religious significance, but it is very uncertain, and all that can really be said is that the inscriptions would be unlikely finds in an ordinary villa. The building may therefore have been a temple of some kind. A rectangular earthwork farther south on Blackheath was perhaps connected with this site.

Another possible religious structure on this side of Londinium was found in 1690 at St Thomas Watering. It seems to have been built, partly at least, of the characteristic large, flat bricks, and associated with it were a 'Janus head' in marble, long since lost, and another sculptured head, which was left in quicksand.[2]

There was probably a villa near Beddington Park Farm, just north of the Wandle, where a room and a hypocaust were found, and another on Coombe Hill, Kingston, where wall foundations and Roman coins were found in the sixteenth century.[3] Immediately west of Orpington Station, flint walls, a threshold, and pavements of coarse red tesserae, presumably of a villa, can still be seen projecting from a bank below the Borough Council Offices.[4]

On the hillside adjoining the Foreign Bird Farm at Warbank, Keston (on the 146 bus route from Bromley South Station) there is a curious walled structure of flint and brick, circular with external buttresses, and about twenty-nine feet in diameter.[5] (*Fig. 36.*) Evidence suggesting a date early in the third century has recently been found and new discoveries have been made outside the structure—notably a cremation in a lead cist, contained in a tomb made by enclosing the space between two of the buttresses with another wall. There is little doubt that the round building itself was a mausoleum belonging to a large villa, about which very little is known, further down the hill. Other burials have been found near by, and a large rectangular tomb with similar walls can be seen to the north of the circular structure. A late Roman sarcophagus

---

[1] *RCHM : RL*, p. 151; *RIB*, 37–39.
[2] Thomas Allen: *History of London*, I, p. 36.
[3] J. Leland: *Itinerary*, 1535–43, pt. 8, 1909 ed., p. 85.
[4] *Arch. Cant.*, LXXI, p. 240; LXXII, p. 210.
[5] Arrangements to visit the Keston site should be made in advance with The Manager, Keston Foreign Bird Farm Ltd., Brambletye, Westerham Road, Keston, Kent (telephone: Farnborough 52351).

Fig. 36 *Roman mausoleum at Keston*

that was found here many years ago can also be seen. This hillside was evidently the burial-place of a family of great importance, and it seems likely that their villa, also, was a grand one—probably larger than the fine villa of Lullingstone that can be visited a few miles to the east. The Keston villa is about twelve miles from Londinium and just over a mile from the Roman road to London from Lewes. It is therefore within easy reach of the capital, and it is tempting to imagine that the circular mausoleum was the burial-place of some high official, who perhaps retired to this pleasant spot, or even used it as a country retreat while still in office.

The absence of luxurious villas within a few miles of Londinium, however, shows that daily commuting from the countryside was not generally practised by the rich and important; and the landowners themselves—whatever the system of tenure—probably mostly preferred to live in the city or Southwark, leaving actual residence on their estates to stewards and farm-servants.

There were also small settlements of native origin, such as the rectangular huts with wattle floors of the second century found on the foreshore at Brentford,[1] and the circular wattle huts of the early Roman period in a similar position below the present high-water-mark at Tilbury.[2] Such settlements were probably mostly very small, the one at Tilbury consisting of three huts. True villages, so numerous in the Greater London area in later times, were almost

[1] *Antiquity*, III, p. 20.
[2] *RCHM: SE. Essex*, p. 38.

non-existent, but there does seem to have been something of this kind at Charlton. It was within a defensive earthwork, now destroyed, which was probably pre-Roman, enclosing $17\frac{1}{2}$ acres on a spur above the marshes about half a mile north-east of Charlton Church. Here there were a number of hut-sites, mostly roughly circular, and the settlement seems to have been occupied from the first century to the end of the third.[1] With this possible exception, the centres of habitation in the London area seem to have consisted mostly of small groups of buildings making up single farmsteads, probably occupied either by family groups or by households of servants working for absentee masters in Londinium.

Farming was not the only concern of these small rural communities: some were also industrial. A notable discovery of 1967 was a kiln-site in the northern part of Highgate Wood, where coarse pottery, such as poppy-head beakers, was made from the local clay, no doubt for the London market. Three kilns were found with a great dump of broken pottery, including many 'wasters' spoilt in manufacture, mostly dating from the latter part of the first century.

Other small potteries were no doubt scattered through Greater London, and a kiln of some kind was found a few years ago in Joyden's Wood, in the Borough of Bexley.[2] Pottery-making on a larger scale seems to have taken place at Brockley Hill near Stanmore, where kilns have been found, probably concerned with the manufacture of reddish-buff kitchen-ware, such as bowls with reeded rims.[3]

The Brockley Hill settlement (Sulloniacae), however, falls into a different category, since it also served as a posting-stage half-way to Verulamium. Similar concentrations of population were to be found on other roads out of Londinium, within a radius of between eleven and eighteen miles from the city: at Staines (Pontes) on the Silchester road (18 miles): at Ewell on Stane Street (12 miles): at Crayford (Noviomagus) on Watling Street ($13\frac{1}{2}$ miles): and to a lesser extent at Little London on the Dunmow road (12 miles). In each case a Roman posting-station was probably the nucleus of its development, but the precise position of the station was no doubt determined by geographical advantages, which may have already

---

[1] *RCHM: RL*, pp. 150–1.
[2] *Arch. Cant.*, LXVIII (1954), p. 170.
[3] *LAMAS Trans.*, N.S., XI (1953), pp. 173–88.

attracted settlers to the neighbourhood.

There is evidence of occupation in Edmonton, where two hut-sites have been found in Churchfield, a short distance to the west of the supposed line of Ermine Street,[1] and also about a mile farther north in Enfield, but these sites are only eight and nine miles respectively from Londinium, and can hardly indicate the proximity of the first posting-station, which remains elusive on this road, as it does on the road to Colchester through Aldgate. On the latter, the name of the station, Durolitum, is known to us, and it *should* be at Romford, but the lack of any definite evidence of Roman occupation there suggests that it was very small indeed. Does the apparent failure of the posting-stations on these two roads to develop into a substantial settlement indicate that both roads declined in importance at an early date? The transfer of the capital to Londinium must have reduced the amount of traffic on the Colchester road very considerably, and there is some evidence that the gateway at Aldgate was comparatively narrow. (*See p. 122.*) A decline of the road to the north through Bishopsgate is more difficult to understand, but it is not mentioned in the Antonine Itinerary—a road-book of about AD 200 surviving through later copies—which gives routes from London to Lincoln (*Iter* VI) and to York (*Iter* VIII) through Verulamium, and therefore via Newgate.

[1] G. R. Gillam: *A Romano-British Site at Edmonton*, privately printed, 1953.

CHAPTER NINE

Life in Roman London

The character of any town owes more to its people than to its geography and architecture, and unless we can reconstruct something of the way of life of Roman Londoners we shall have a very incomplete picture of their city. Fortunately it is not difficult to do so, for a wealth of evidence has survived; and the visitor to the London and Guildhall Museums, and to the Roman Britain section of the British Museum, will make a direct contact with the very things that these ancient Londoners knew and handled.

The population of the earliest Roman London has been estimated on the basis of the combined casualty figure for Boudicca's destruction of Camulodunum, Londinium and Verulamium, given by Tacitus as 70,000. Allowing for exaggeration, this suggests a population of about 15,000 each for Camulodunum and Verulamium and 30,000 for Londinium.[1] Comparison of the acreage of the *colonia* at Colchester with that of *coloniae* elsewhere for which figures are available also suggests a population of about 15,000 for that city, so this estimate for the first London may not be far out. If so, it seems likely that the number of inhabitants eventually increased with the further development of London to at least 45,000.[2]

Who were these Roman Londoners? Romans of Italian origin must have formed only a small part of the ruling official class, in which Roman citizens of Gaulish descent, like Classicianus himself, were no doubt more numerous, and there were others of Spanish or even North African origin. Some probably came from provinces

[1] *Britannia*, p. 261.
[2] A. Birley: *Life in Roman Britain*, 1964, pp. 66–7.

farther east, since there were almost certainly worshippers from Danubian lands in the Walbrook Mithraeum, and these are more likely to have been soldiers or officials than traders. (*See pp. 195–6.*) In due course native-born Britons, also, would have aspired to positions in the provincial hierarchy, so that the upper class of Londinium, though politically and culturally completely Roman, must have been a constantly changing racial mixture.

Below the official establishment was the most conspicuous class of Roman Londoners, the merchants and financiers who were specially mentioned by Tacitus. These also were cosmopolitan and they included immigrants from the eastern half of the Empire—men such as Aulus Alfidius Olussa, who was born in Athens, and whose tombstone, found on Tower Hill, is in the British Museum.[1] Others, such as Rufus, son of Callisunus, whose letter concerning his business interests in Londinium has survived on a wooden writing-tablet,[2] were of Celtic origin. Olussa was a Roman citizen; Rufus was not, but he was evidently a man of substance.

Then there was the large class of small tradesmen and craftsmen, probably mostly of British or Gaulish origin. Many of these were probably freedmen, like the two partners whose stamp has been found on tiles from Bishopsgate (in the London Museum), Bush Lane (Guildhall Museum), and from Whitehall. Their names suggest that they were both given their freedom by the same master, *D(ecimus) M. . . . .*[3] From marks on goods found in London and probably—though not certainly—made there, we know the names of a cutler, Basilis or Basilius (with knives in the London and British Museums); tool-makers, Aprilis, Martinus (with chisels in Guildhall Museum) and Titulus (with an awl in the London Museum); and curriers, Burdonius and Verus (with pieces of marked leather in Guildhall Museum). A more curious trade was that of C. Silvius Tetricus, a Roman citizen of Gaulish origin, who made ointments for various eye troubles. His stone stamp, beautifully lettered with labels for four of these, found in Upper Thames Street, can be seen in Guildhall Museum. (*Fig. 37.*) It was presumably either used directly on the cake of ointment or, more probably, on the wax sealing of the package that contained it.

At the bottom of the social ladder were the slaves, probably mostly Britons—those taken prisoner in the wars of conquest, and

[1] *RIB*, **9**. It is probably of the 1st century.
[2] In the British Museum. See also p. 86 and fn.
[3] *JRS*, LIV (1964), p. 183, no. 29; LVI (1966), p. 222, no. 29.

Fig. 37 *Stone stamp for eye ointments made*
by C. Silvius Tetricus, found in Upper Thames Street

their descendants; but skilled slaves would also certainly have been imported for special kinds of work. They were not all employed in menial tasks: some, like Anencletus, slave of the Provincial Council, did clerical work of an official character; others, like Epillicus, the head servant of Rufus, son of Callisunus, were trusted stewards to whom a considerable amount of responsibility was given. The tone of Rufus' letter to Epillicus and his fellow-slaves, while clearly that of a master, is friendly and even courteous. (*See p. 86.*)

Slaves in the kind of employment for which they would have been used in Londinium—as domestic servants, craftsmen and clerks—were usually fairly well treated, and had a reasonable chance of achieving their freedom. Nevertheless, they sometimes ran away, like the slave mentioned in a letter written in ink on a wooden tablet that was found in a well or pit on the site of Temple Court, Queen Victoria Street. It was apparently sent from Rochester (Durobrivae) to a correspondent in London, and tantalizing fragments of it were legible when it was first found. This was not a simple case of a flight to freedom, however, for the boy seems to have absconded with something that he should perhaps have brought to London.[1]

The letters described are written in Latin, which must have been the only common language of the cosmopolitan population of Roman London. The view of philologists is that Latin was very little spoken in Roman Britain as a whole, although it was used by the literate for writing. In London, however, spoken Latin must have been in general use both in official and commercial circles, and its

---

[1] Translated by Professor E. G. Turner and Professor Otto Skutsch in *JRS*, L (1960), pp. 108–11. The pieces of wooden tablet are in Guildhall Museum, but unfortunately the ink vanished in the course of the conservation of the wood.

convenience as a *lingua franca* in such a mixed population probably resulted in its percolation down to the lower levels of society.

The innumerable *graffiti* testify not only to the familiarity of written Latin but also to the prevalence of literacy at such levels. Usually, it is true, *graffiti* are of the simplest possible character—such as a name, often abbreviated, scratched on a pot that may have contained a workman's lunch. Occasionally, however, we find something more elaborate in circumstances that suggest quite a humble authorship. There is a famous tile in Guildhall Museum, which has the following sentence scratched on it:

> *Austalis dibus XIII vagatur sib(i) cotidim*

This can be translated:

> 'For the last fortnight Austalis has been wandering off on his own every day.' (*Fig. 38.*)

Fig. 38 *Tile with inscription scratched on before firing, commenting on the behaviour of Austalis, found in Warwick Lane*

Since the tile was scratched before firing, it is generally assumed that one of the brick-makers was responsible, and that he was writing about one of his fellow-workers. The usual explanation is that he was complaining about the truant, who was not doing his fair share of the work; and the standard witticism is that this is the first recorded instance of absenteeism by a British workman. It is as likely to be a joke as a case of tale-telling, however; and I prefer to believe that there was a romantic explanation for the disappearances of Austalis, and that he was being teased accordingly by his friends.

Tacitus tells us that thanks to the Romanizing policy pursued by his father-in-law, Agricola, as Governor of Britain, the toga was to be seen everywhere. This was the distinctive formal dress of the Roman—a voluminous robe of fine white wool, not quite semicircular when laid flat, with its straight edge about six yards long. It was hung over the left shoulder with the straight edge nearest the centre of the body, and the point nearly touching the ground in front. The rest was then carefully draped round the wearer, so that the other point almost touched the ground behind. It was not easy to put it on properly, and even more difficult to wear when engaged in any kind of activity; it was expensive to buy in the first instance, and expensive to maintain in the state of immaculate whiteness that was required. It had therefore that quality which is necessary for all formal dress—the glamour of privilege. In this case, however, it was not merely the privilege of wealth and leisure, but also of the special rights and dignity of Roman citizenship. To some extent this strong appeal must have offset the manifest disadvantages of the toga—one of the least practical dresses that could be devised for a wet and muddy town in Britain.

A tombstone in Guildhall Museum shows in relief a gentleman wearing a voluminous robe that is usually described as a toga, but has also been called a *pallium*—a cloak made from a rectangular cloth.[1] (*Fig. 39.*) It is draped round the wearer covering his right arm, and is bunched up in his left hand to lift the trailing edge clear of the ground. The tombstone is of imported marble, and as its history is unknown it is somewhat suspect as a find of Roman London. On the other hand the carving is decidedly provincial, and the formal treatment of the folds of drapery almost as a pattern is British in style. It can at any rate be taken as an illustration of

[1] J. M. C. Toynbee: *Art in Britain under the Romans*, p. 198.

Fig. 39 *Tombstone showing man
with toga and small boy*

the more formal dress that might have been seen in Londinium.
The ordinary costume of a Roman Londoner about his everyday
business, however, is better represented by the clothes worn by the
small boy who accompanies the dignified robed figure in the relief.
The boy, who may be a slave, wears a short-sleeved or sleeveless
tunic reaching to his knees, and over this has a very short cloak,
which would probably have been fastened with a brooch-like pin
at the shoulder. No hood can be seen, but it is probable that one
was attached to the back and could be pulled over the head in bad
weather.

Fragments of cloth have sometimes been found, preserved in
waterlogged deposits such as the stream-bed of the Walbrook, but
the only articles of apparel that have survived reasonably complete
in London have been those made of leather. Shoes, mostly a form of
open sandal, can be seen in both the London and Guildhall
Museums. The commonest type is a slipper, the sole of which
has a row of loops on each side, skilfully cut from a single piece of
leather. It was fastened by means of a thong, which criss-crossed
between the loops on one side and those on the other, and was tied

round the ankle. Another type of open sandal has a network of thongs, to fit over the toes and round the ankle, sometimes forming a lattice pattern. There are also shoes with an elaborate ornamentation of small perforations cut in the uppers, and these, likewise, were often fastened by lacing through a row of loops on each side. Stout boots were also worn, but are rarely found complete, since the upper was a separate piece of leather, which tended to break away from the sole. The soles with heavy hob-nails, sometimes arranged in a pattern, are common in all the collections from Roman London.

The most interesting leather object found in London, however, is a pair of very brief trunks, found deep in the silt filling of a timber-lined well on the site of the Bank of London and South America in Queen Street. It is now exhibited in Guildhall Museum. (*Fig. 40.*) The well was entirely filled before the end of the first

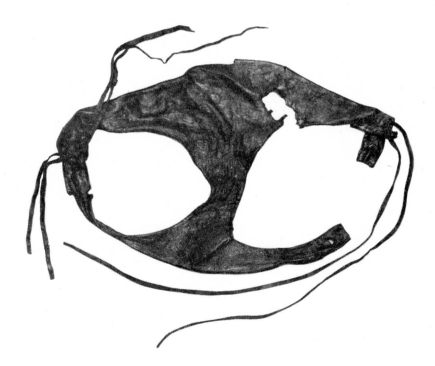

Fig. 40 *Leather 'bikini' trunks, from 1st-century well, Queen Street*

153

century, as is shown by the pottery found in it, so the garment was lost in the first fifty years of London's existence. It is of the simplest possible character, but is beautifully made, with a hem that is invisible from the outside, since the stitches go only half-way through the leather. From its shape it must have been worn by a girl, but a very small, slim one, little more than a child.

The trunks soon acquired the nickname of 'the Roman bikini', and were compared with those worn with an equally abbreviated upper garment by girls represented on a late Roman mosaic pavement in the palatial Roman villa at Piazza Armerina in Sicily. These 'bikini' girls are either engaged in some kind of athletic contest or are dancing-girls giving an entertainment. The mosaic does not provide a good parallel for our 'bikini', however, because of its fourth-century date, which is almost as remote from the period of the London garment as our own times are from those of Queen Elizabeth I. A better parallel is provided by a small bronze figure that used to be in the Museum at Rennes in Brittany. This represents a girl wearing trunks very much more like ours, and is probably much nearer the same date. As in the London 'bikini', the fastening is by means of long laces, which are tied on the hips on each side. The method by which the laces are pulled through holes in the garment to enclose the thigh and are then knotted on the hip, can be clearly seen on the London trunks, in which one side is unfastened, but the other remains tied with the knot that was made nearly nineteen centuries ago. This, incidentally, is a granny.

The Rennes girl wears no upper garment, but has clog-like sandals and curious bracers, presumably of leather, round her knees. The purpose of these must have been to resist strain, so it may be suspected that the trunks were not just a modesty garment but fulfilled the same purpose. The girl is standing in rather a curious attitude, as if about to do something difficult, and the suggestion has been made that she is an acrobatic dancer. On this analogy, therefore, it seems likely that the leather trunks in Guildhall Museum belonged to a girl performer, but the circumstances in which she lost them in the well can only be guessed.

Brooches in great variety were worn as dress-fastenings by both sexes. They were of two main types, one consisting of a pin sliding upon an open ring—the penannular type—which is less common in London, and the other designed on the same principle as the safety-pin. Many different forms of the latter are found, some simple and others very elaborate. They are mostly made of bronze, and are sometimes decorated with enamel of blue, red, green, yellow or white—often with more than one colour. Some were imported from the Continent, especially Belgium, but many types were made in Britain. Animal, bird and fish forms are common. Some brooches have a portion of chain attached, and these were probably worn in pairs, linked by the chain, one on each shoulder.

Bracelets and armlets of bronze and occasionally silver are found; and in later Roman times they were also made of Kimmeridge shale and jet from Whitby. Finger-rings of gold, bronze, iron, jet and glass were worn, and the metal rings often have an intaglio design for use as a seal, engraved on the metal itself or on an inset stone, genuine or imitated in paste. On a little bronze ring in Guildhall Museum there is a curious bearded head, and spaced round the wire hoop are the letters A–M–I–C–A ('sweetheart'). Perhaps the love affair of its owner ended in disillusionment, for the ring was eventually thrown or dropped into the stream of the Walbrook.

The great majority of these London finds were in fact found either in the ancient stream-bed or in the flood-deposits that from time to time covered its banks; and, through the action of various organic acids that occurred there, they have mostly been preserved in a completely uncorroded condition. Bronze and brass objects when first recovered shone like gold, as no doubt they did when they were worn, but they have since gradually become tarnished. The associated coins show that these finds belong mostly to the period between the Conquest and about AD 160,[1] and for this time they give us a remarkably detailed picture of life in Roman London.

Beads of glass, paste, jet and chalcedony, mostly of the ribbed variety, have been found in London; and a neck-ornament of a distinctively Celtic type, found in the Walbrook valley, can be seen in Guildhall Museum. This is a torque, consisting of a rod of bronze with knobbed ends, which was curved to fit round the neck. Ear-rings are rare, but there are examples—both of gold—in the British Museum and Guildhall Museum.

Ladies' hair-pins in bone, jet, bronze and silver are common, and sometimes have elaborate terminals. Representations of hands holding fruit were especially popular and can be found in all three of the great London collections. Ladies' hair-fashions changed as frequently as they do today, but were all based on long hair, so that

[1] R. Merrifield: 'Coins from the Bed of the Walbrook, and their Significance', in *Ant. Journ.* XLII, 1962, pp. 38–52.

Fig. 42 *Bronze toilet set from the Walbrook, Bucklersbury House site*

Fig. 41 *Top of bone hair-pin, representing lady with elaborate hairstyle of late 1st century*

hair-pins were always in demand. A complicated hair-style that was in vogue in the latter part of the first century is represented on the terminal of one of the bone hair-pins in Guildhall Museum. This shows the bust of a lady with her hair standing up in a fan-like arrangement in front, obviously held in position by a row of hair-pins, the tips of which can be clearly seen. (*Fig. 41.*)

Ladies then as now devoted a considerable amount of attention to their toilet. Make-up and perfume were used, as we know from the classical writers, and these were no doubt contained in the long-necked phials and flasks, sometimes of pottery but more usually of glass, which are frequently found. They were extracted and applied by means of little spoon-like instruments of bronze, which are very common indeed in London. These were also used for surgical purposes, however, and it is usually impossible to determine whether a particular example was a surgical or toilet instrument. Tweezers, also, could be used for both purposes, but the little sets of three or more bronze implements attached together to a ring or chatelaine were evidently carried by ladies for use in their toilet. (*Fig. 42.*) They usually consist of a pair of tweezers for plucking eyebrows and removing other unwanted hair, an instrument for cleaning the finger-nails, and a little spoon-like implement. The last is often described unromantically by archaeologists as an 'ear-scoop', but is very like the small instrument included in most modern manicure sets for pushing back the cuticle.

Since ornaments and knick-knacks of cheap material were so common in Roman London, it seems likely that only the poorest were unable to afford them. Then as now, girls of all classes probably made some attempt to keep up with fashion and eagerly acquired the latest trinkets.

Mingling with the civilians in the streets of Londinium there was probably nearly always a fair sprinkling of soldiers. They included men from all the British legions, seconded for special duties on the staff of the governor or merely in transit. The appearance and dress of such a soldier can be seen in the large relief in Guildhall Museum. (*Fig. 43*.) Originally from a funerary monument of early date—not later than the early second century—it was found re-used as building

Fig. 43 *Figure in high relief of a Roman soldier, originally from a monument in the cemetery, found re-used as building material in a bastion of the city wall in Camomile Street*

material in the core of the Camomile Street bastion.[1] The figure is wearing a tunic and cloak, and round his neck has a scarf to prevent chafing by a cuirass. No other armour can be seen, but he has his short sword, slung high on the right side, and another military touch is the brass-studded strap terminating in a crescent-shaped ornament that hangs from his belt. Attached to a strap in his left hand is a case of writing-tablets, showing that his duties were partly clerical. Similar writing-cases are shown elsewhere in the hands of junior officers, such as the *optio*, understudy to a centurion, the *signifer*, standard-bearer, and even the more senior *aquilifer*, bearer of the sacred eagle. The London soldier may have occupied any of these positions, for his right hand, which would have held the appropriate emblem of office, is missing. In the context of the provincial capital, however, there is a strong probability that he was a junior officer seconded from his legion to the headquarters staff.

This sculpture and all the military inscriptions found in London are from the tombs of legionaries, but there is also in Guildhall Museum a gravestone of an auxiliary soldier, presumably found in London although there is no record of its discovery. He is represented in low relief, wearing a helmet, cloak and tunic, and carrying the spear and oval shield of an auxiliary infantryman. This soldier may have died while in transit in London, but may equally well have served in the governor's bodyguard.

The commonest weapons found in London are spearheads, such as were normally used by auxiliaries, but were apparently sometimes also carried by legionaries (whose standard equipment in war was the *pilum* or javelin with a long, straight head). Some of these weapons may have been hunting-spears, but most are probably military; and one in Guildhall Museum, found in a well of the late first century, has an inscription punched in dots, indicating that it belonged to a century commanded by a centurion named Ver(us) Vict(or). Dr Graham Webster has pointed out that troops closely connected with the government were likely to have carried spears as symbols of office.

There is a fine legionary dagger, with the iron frame of its sheath, in the London Museum, and another in Guildhall Museum, both from the Walbrook. Another dagger-blade of a different type, in Guildhall Museum, was probably intended for practice only, as the point is extremely blunt.

[1] J. E. Price: *On a Bastion of London Wall*, 1880, pp. 30 ff.

The finest weapon from the London area, however, is the legionary sword from the Thames at Fulham, with an embossed bronze scabbard on which is a representation of Romulus and Remus. (*See p. 21.*) This is in the British Museum, as also is a legionary helmet with the names of four successive owners on the neck-guard. It comes from London, and from its condition is presumably from the Thames or Walbrook, but the find-spot is not recorded. Both the sword and helmet are of early date, however, and are more likely to have been lost during the campaign of AD 43 than after the establishment of Londinium.

Other military finds from London include a bronze shield-boss (London Museum), iron heads of ballista bolts and an arrowhead, pieces of bone from composite bows, fragments of armour, including chain mail, and various fastenings and ornaments from soldiers' uniforms (Guildhall Museum). Most of these are from the Walbrook.

No doubt many soldiers finally settled down in London or the London area when their period of service was over. One of these presumably owned the discharge certificate, inscribed on bronze and dated AD 105, which was found in Sydenham and is now in the British Museum (not exhibited).

An account of the surviving remains of some of the houses and other buildings of the Roman city has been given in Chapter 6, but it must be remembered that not all of the inhabitants lived in large, solidly built ragstone mansions with mosaic floors and hypocaust heating. More numerous were the humbler houses and shops built of clay, usually on a timber framework, and in the earlier period Londinium consisted almost entirely of such buildings. Their floors were often of earth or clay, but sometimes also of mortar, concrete or coarse red tesserae. Even these poorer buildings, however, frequently had painted wall-plaster—usually, it must be admitted, of crude design and garish colours. Most Roman Londoners lived against a domestic background of blood-red or mustard-yellow, which perhaps gave an illusion of warmth to those who were unable to afford the luxury of central heating, and whose sole protection against the rigours of a cold, damp climate was probably a simple brazier. Even in the mansions of the rich only a few of the rooms seem to have been heated by a hypocaust system, so that comfort in winter was the exception rather than the rule.

The roofs of the humbler houses were probably mostly of thatch, but the more substantial buildings had overlapping roof-tiles of a type that is still commonly used in Italy and southern France.

Window-glass was used, but is not nearly so common as might be expected, and it is unlikely that the poorer houses were equipped with it. The alternative was probably a wooden shutter, which gave a choice between warmth and daylight.

The usual source of internal artificial lighting was the oil-lamp. Candlesticks of iron, bronze or pottery also occur, as well as portions of elaborate bronze candelabra, but these are much less abundant than the little moulded terra-cotta lamps, which are often elaborately ornamented. In this London was perhaps exceptional in Roman Britain,[1] probably because the imported olive-oil used as fuel was more easily obtainable there than in the remoter parts of the province. Pottery lamp-fillers and lamp-holders—trays for holding and carrying the hot lamp—are also common. Bronze and iron lamps of various types are represented in the London and Guildhall Museums, but these are much rarer than those of pottery. Torches were no doubt also used, especially out of doors, but of this we have no direct evidence from London.

Evidence for the furniture used in the homes of Roman London is also indirect, but a good idea of it can be obtained from Gaulish funerary reliefs representing domestic scenes, supplemented by fragmentary remains from other parts of the country.[2] Smaller household equipment of pottery, glass and metal, however, can be seen in abundance, and there are even a few objects of wood, which have survived in waterlogged conditions.

From the first-century well in Queen Street, where the leather trunks were found, comes a wooden ladder in Guildhall Museum, probably lost because the depth of the well was underestimated when an attempt was made to clear the silt. From the same well there is a wooden spoon or scoop, which looks (after treatment and bleaching to restore the natural colour) as if it had been bought in Woolworth's only a few weeks ago. This also is in Guildhall Museum. A wooden dipper from the bottom of this well is shown with other finds from the site in the board-room of the Bank of London and South America in Queen Street, and can sometimes be seen by special permission.

A fine bronze 'kettle' or cooking-pot from another early well, underlying the basilica in Cornhill, is exhibited in the London Museum (*Fig. 44*), and there are frying-pans and saucepans, some

[1] Sheppard Frere (in *Britannia*, 1967, p. 290, fn.) states that lamps are not common in Britain, even in the towns, and that the candle probably remained the chief source of artificial light.
[2] For this, the reader is referred to Miss J. Liversidge's book, *Furniture in Roman Britain*, 1955.

Fig. 44 *Bronze 'kettle' and jug from a 1st-century well in Cornhill*

with makers' names on the handles, in both of the great London collections. Also used in the preparation of food were the mixing-bowls of rather coarse grey or buff pottery called *mortaria*. These are studded with coarse grit on the inner surface and have a spout for pouring out the contents. Most kitchens probably had several of these, and no doubt they served a variety of purposes. They evidently received rather rough treatment, and are commonly found with a hole worn in the bottom. One of the aims of the Roman *haute cuisine* seems to have been to produce dishes that gave no visible indication of their original ingredients,[1] and something of the same fashion may have descended to the humblest households.

Fig. 45 *Roman knives from the Walbrook*

[1] J. Carcopino: *Daily Life in Ancient Rome*, Penguin translation, 1956, p. 271.

The larders of Roman London were well equipped with storage vessels of various kinds. Pottery containers range in size from small pots, used for honey and other preserves, to huge jars of coarse ware, which were probably used for the storage of grain—like one in Guildhall Museum that is 2 ft. 5 in. high, with a maximum diameter of about 2 ft. 6 in. Square glass bottles with handles were used for liquids such as oil, vinegar and probably also the ubiquitous fish-sauce that played such an important part in Roman cooking. This was a supremely practical shape, since the bottles could be closely packed on a shelf with no wastage of space. It is therefore surprising that it had a fairly short life, and apparently ceased to be used before the end of the second century.

Knives of many forms and sizes are common: they range from great butchers' implements with triangular blades to small and rather dainty ones, which were probably used at table. (*Fig. 45.*)

Spoons also can be seen in the museum collections. These are of bronze, pewter and bone, but rich people would have used silver spoons, which are known from hoards elsewhere. No London example seems to have been recorded, however, and they probably mostly ended in the melting-pot. A pewter spoon in Guildhall Museum has a representation of three fishes on the bowl. It has been suggested that this may be an example of Christian symbolism, but it is more likely that the reference is purely gastronomic. A special type of spoon, which is commoner than any other, is the *cochleare*, which has a small, round bowl and a handle tapering to a point. It was used for eating eggs, shell-fish and snails, and the pointed end was no doubt very useful for winkling out the last delicious little piece of the snail from its shell.

In the richest houses food was served in vessels of silver, but the odds against the survival of these are very great, and we have none from Roman London. The Mildenhall Treasure in the British Museum is a magnificent example of late Roman silver tableware, and no doubt sets equally fine were to be seen in Londinium. The less wealthy made do with vessels of bronze or pewter, and a number of examples of these have been recovered, mostly from wells or from the Walbrook. A small dish and a cup of bronze, the latter with inlaid decoration, are shown in Guildhall Museum. With them is the handle of a bronze wine-jug, which is elaborately decorated with a representation in relief of Ganymede being carried off by the eagle. The London Museum has a complete bronze jug of early type from the same well as the cooking-pot. (*See fig. 44.*), and two jugs from Threadneedle Street, one with a female bust and the other with a fine mask of Oceanus at the base of the handle. Both museums have a pewter jug and cup, and there are in Guildhall Museum two pewter plates from the Walbrook, which are different in form from the usual late Roman plates in this material found elsewhere. It is suspected that they may be earlier, and the fairly frequent occurrence of pewter objects among Walbrook finds, which mostly belong to the period before AD 160, is difficult to reconcile with the theory that pewter was a Romano-British invention of the mid-third century.[1]

Glass drinking-vessels of fine quality were used by those who could afford them, and a delicate beaker of egg-shell thinness can be seen in Guildhall Museum. In the same case is a superb drinking-cup of white glass with two exquisitely cut handles—in form a copy of an Augustan type of silver cup. This was an import from the east and must have been a very costly object. (*See p. 85.*) Like so many of the treasures found in London it comes from a rubbish-pit—in this case a superior timber-lined affair like a shallow well, on the site of St Swithin's House, Walbrook. This evidently belonged to a rich household of the first century, and it contained more than one piece of fine glass. Among them is another exceptional vessel—a *rhyton* or drinking-horn of similar glass, which presumably came from the same source. Both vessels are of course fragmentary, and were no doubt thrown away because they were broken. One hopes that they survived to give pleasure for a few years at least after their long sea-voyage, before they found their way into the rubbish-hole.

About the end of the first century, cut glass with facetted decoration became popular, and both the London and Guildhall Museums have beakers ornamented in this way. A vessel in the latter collection has a fantastic decoration of raised rosettes and other figures produced by cutting.

Fine glass of this kind must have been expensive, but moulded bowls, with vertical pillars to imitate the fluting of metal prototypes, are so numerous in the first century that they are likely to have been within the reach of the average household. They are mostly of the ordinary bluish-green glass, but beautiful coloured examples, sometimes variegated, are also found, and a pillar-moulded bowl of dark-blue glass can be seen in Guildhall Museum.

[1] As suggested by C. A. Peal: 'Romano-British Pewter Plates and Dishes', in *Proc. Camb. Ant. Soc.*, LX (1967), p. 19.

Also at a price that could be afforded by the average family, at least for its best table-ware, was the beautifully finished glossy red pottery from Gaul. If you could not afford silver you used bronze, which looked like gold; but if a complete service of bronze were also unattainable, the next best thing was this handsome ware of coral red—just as shiny as any metal and with shapes as clean-cut as the precious vessels of the very rich. If you admired the elaborately chased ornamentation with which the silversmith embellished his costly bowls, this also could be supplied by the Gaulish potter for very little more than the price of his plain wares. You could have floral designs, representations of classical legends, hunting scenes, gladiatorial combats or even activities in brothels—all according to taste. The only drawback was that you might find an identical pattern on your friend's dinner-table, since these vessels were produced in large numbers from moulds.

This fine ware from Gaul, usually known as samian ware (from an early misnomer that is too firmly established to be discarded), has been closely studied by archaeologists, who find it invaluable for purposes of dating. The actual potters can often be identified, not only from their names stamped or moulded on their products, but also from their distinctive styles of decoration when the name is absent. In most cases, the approximate duration of a potter's activities and the place of his factory is known. Changes of fashion, both in shape and decoration, are also helpful. In general, the early ware from South Gaul is of the finest quality, and the later products of Central and Eastern Gaul eventually deteriorate into great coarseness of form and crudity of decoration. Some very fine pots were, however, made in Central Gaul late in the second century, and one of these, found in Southwark, can be seen in Guildhall Museum. It is decorated in very high relief by applying separate moulded ornaments, representing Cupids stalking deer and confronting boars. (*Fig. 46.*)

Civil war and barbarian invasions in Gaul put an end to the production of samian ware in the third century, and its place as the best table-ware of Roman London was taken by glossy, dark drinking-vessels from the Rhineland, sometimes decorated with mottoes in white slip, and by British pottery of similar type, which was made in the Nene Valley of Northamptonshire and elsewhere. This was decorated freehand with semi-liquid clay, in very much the same way as icing is applied to a cake. Representations of hunting scenes with running animals were popular, and the old

Fig. 46 *Roman samian vase with moulded decoration in high relief, found in Southwark, late 2nd century*

Fig. 47 *Roman beaker of Nene Valley type, decorated freehand with running stag, found in Jewry Street*

M

Celtic love of flowing curves and scrolls came to life again. (*Fig. 47.*) The decoration of each beaker or cup was individually produced by hand, and therefore has a stronger appeal to us today than the mass-produced moulded decoration of samian ware.

Two other types of fine table-ware deserve special mention. One was perhaps the most effective of all substitutes in pottery for bronze, since it was not only made in the forms of metal vessels, but the surface was given a convincingly metallic lustre by dusting with mica. This was fairly common in Roman London in the latter part of the first and the early second century, and some may have been made locally, as wasters (pots spoiled in manufacture) are said to have been found in Copthall Close.[1] Very much rarer were the first-century wares with green or brown lead glaze, small fragments of which can look disconcertingly like medieval or even seventeenth-century pottery. One kind came from St Rémy in Central Gaul, but the sources of the others have not yet been discovered.

To satisfy the needs of a large urban community which, as we have seen, demanded much more than the bare necessities of life, a variety of service-trades and crafts were required. Many households undoubtedly ground their own corn with the small hand-querns that are often found, and therefore, no doubt, baked their own bread. There was at least one baker's establishment that did this work on a large scale, however, like those found in Pompeii and Ostia. It probably stood on the banks of the Walbrook, on a site now occupied by the National Provincial Bank in Prince's Street, since it was here that the massive upper stone of one of its mills was found. This—now in Guildhall Museum—is exactly like the millstones still standing in the baker's yard in Pompeii. It fitted over a conical lower stone and was turned by means of poles, which passed through the holes in the sides and were attached to a horse or donkey.

As might be expected, few traces have survived of the numerous merchants in provisions of various kinds, apart from the steelyards, which were probably used for weighing out foodstuffs in their shops and stalls. This was an ingenious device consisting of a bar marked with a graduated scale and fixed to a hook, which served as a fulcrum. The object to be weighed was attached to another hook and a weight was moved along the bar until the latter balanced

---

[1] Guildhall Library Report, 1936, pp. 14–15. The finds from Copthall Close are not now in Guildhall Museum, but in the collection there is an undoubted waster from an unknown site in the City.

horizontally. Its position on the scale then indicated the weight of the object. By reversing the bar and using another hook as the fulcrum a different scale of weights on the opposite side could be used. A good example, found a few years ago while tunnelling through the Walbrook at the Bank Underground Station, can be seen in Guildhall Museum. The sliding weights were often in the form of the head or bust of a human being or deity, and there is one in the London Museum representing the goddess Isis. Balances were also used, and the London Museum has an interesting example of a combined steelyard and balance, in which the steelyard principle of a sliding weight was used on one arm of the balance to measure fractional weights below half an ounce (twelve scruples).

Guildhall Museum is particularly rich in craftsmen's tools, nearly all found in the Walbrook. They are free from rust, owing to the action of organic acids in the waterlogged gravel and silt, and are mostly still serviceable—or would be if they were re-sharpened. Builders and stone-masons left behind in the stream their picks, trowels, points, dividers and a lewising-tool—used for making an under-cut groove in a block of stone for the attachment of a lewis, by which it could be hoisted. (*See p. 113.*) Plasterers left their small-tools; carpenters their chisels, draw-knives, bits, scribing-awls and drills. Most fascinating of all are their neat folding foot-rules of brass, 11·6 inches in length (the Roman *pes*) and marked in quarters (*palmae*), twelfths (*unciae*) and sixteenths (*digiti*). When extended the rule is kept rigid by a small clamp, which locks on a stud.

The most striking characteristic of all these tools is their remarkable similarity to those in use today. This has been demonstrated in Guildhall Museum by showing the modern tool beside its ancient counterparts. It is clear that the modern handicraftman, whether in wood, stone, metal or leather, would find himself perfectly at home if he could be transported to the workshops of Roman London.

CHAPTER TEN

Religion in Roman London

The deities of Roman London were as diverse as its people, as might be expected in a city where so many cultural traditions met and mingled. The official attitude of the rulers was one of tolerance, except where religion impinged on politics. Only those religions that seemed to conflict with whole-hearted loyalty to the Roman State were suspect, and persecutions arose, not from Roman bigotry, but from the inability of those who worshipped an exclusive God to accept the religious content of Roman patriotism.

The official state religion was the worship of the Capitoline deities, Jupiter, Juno and Minerva, who would certainly have had a temple in the centre of London when it became the capital. This was the cult of Roman citizens, and it made few, if any, demands on unenfranchised provincials. It was quite otherwise with the newer state cult of Emperor-worship, which was intended to unite all who were ruled by Rome, and to provide a focal point for their loyalties. What was worshipped by the Romans was not the living Emperor, but his divinity (*numen*), and he was not officially regarded as a god until after his death. These theological subtleties were not always understood by provincials, and initially a more personal cult of Claudius seems to have been established at Camulodunum. The Britons were compelled to do more than pay lip-service to the cult: each tribe or *civitas* had to send delegates to the provincial council, whose principal function was to attend the annual ceremonies of Emperor-worship. One of them was elected as high priest for the year, and was obliged to provide a costly festival. This took place initially at Camulodunum, but there seems little doubt that it was transferred to Londinium, where a slave of the provincial council evidently lived, and where a great shrine was dedicated to the divinity of the Emperor, significantly not by any individual or local administration, but by the Province of Britain. (*See p. 75.*) The two inscriptions that testify to this are both of early date, and it is likely that the cult centre was transferred with the administration of the province after the suppression of Boudicca's revolt.

All this was a matter of loyalty rather than religion, as was the military cult, which would have been centred on the shrine in the headquarters building of the fort, where the sacred standards were kept. Here the guardian spirit of the Emperor was honoured, together with Capitoline Jupiter if, as is likely, the fort housed legionaries, since these were Roman citizens.

In the worship of pagan gods there was little to divide Romans from Britons, once the more gruesome barbaric rites had been suppressed or toned down. The Celtic peoples worshipped rather vague nature spirits, often local in character, and the methodical Roman mind was soon busy systematizing these and equating them with familiar deities. Under the influence of Roman art they took on human form, in which they were often distinguishable from their Mediterranean analogues only by some unfamiliar attribute or by the addition of an outlandish local name to an inscription. There were other native deities who defied translation into the standard types of classical mythology, and materialized in representational art into part-animal or multiple forms, but these were equally acceptable.

As might be expected, in cosmopolitan London the native elements are less conspicuous than in the north and west of Britain. The cult of the Celtic mother-goddess, however, was certainly popular, and her assimilation into one of the Mediterranean mother-goddess types was prevented by the Celtic insistence on embodying her in triplicate, to express some fundamental idea of the threefold power of her divinity. This representation is, however, Gaulish in origin, and the cult is by no means purely British. One of the temples of the trio of mother-goddesses probably stood near St Olave's Church, Hart Street, where their cult figures, now in Guildhall Museum, were found. They are represented in a limestone relief as three respectably draped and seated matrons— unfortunately with their upper portions missing—each with a baskets of fruits on her lap, as a symbol of fertility and abundance.

In the same museum is an inscription from Budge Row:

MATR[IBVS] VICINIA DE SVO RES[TITVIT]

'to the Mother-Goddesses the district restored (this shrine) at its own expense.'[1] (*See fig. 21, p. 93.*)

There is also a small plaque of tin (formerly thought to be silver) with a representation in repoussé of the mother-goddesses, found in Moorgate and now in the London Museum. It shows the three goddesses sitting between two columns and beneath a triple arch, holding bowls on their laps and with branch-like objects in their left hands. The plaque is evidently votive, and may have been deposited in a shrine beside one of the streamlets feeding the Walbrook from the west. Single representations of a mother-goddess seated in a basket chair and suckling one or two infants are also found, and can be seen in both the London and Guildhall Museums. These are pipe-clay figurines imported from Central Gaul, and they were probably kept in small domestic shrines or used as votive offerings in temples. They may have been charms to assist in childbirth rather than cult-figures.

The few other purely Celtic religious emblems found in London are almost certainly merely amulets rather than indications of the practice of native cults. They include a small bronze wheel, the emblem of Taranis, the Celtic divine smith and thunder-god, from the Walbrook in Guildhall Museum. In the same collection is a strange double head from Lothbury carved in native style from the base of an antler, the burr of which forms the fringe of hair and beard of one face, and the hair alone of the other. There are two holes for attachment, and it was probably worn as a charm. This is not the Roman Janus, though there may be some influence from representations of the two-faced god of doorways and of beginnings. Double and triple heads are well known, however, as purely Celtic religious symbols, and the basic element seems to be the human head, regarded by all Celtic peoples as the seat of supernatural power, which is emphasized by double or triple representation.[2]

Mediterranean deities seem on the face of it to be predominant in Londinium, but in this, as we shall see, things may not always be quite as they appear. A fine stone altar with a relief of Diana is preserved in Goldsmiths' Hall, Foster Lane, where it was found. The goddess is represented as a slim young huntress, wearing a

---

[1] *RIB*, 2.
[2] Anne Ross: *Pagan Celtic Britain*, 1967, pp. 73–81.

short, belted tunic, with a bow in one hand, and in the act of pulling an arrow from a quiver on her shoulder with the other. A dog is sitting at her feet, looking up at her. The carving is provincial in workmanship, but the style is classical, and there seems no good reason for supposing that anyone but the Italian goddess is represented. A suggestion to the contrary has been made, however,[1] and Diana was probably sometimes identified with local deities of wild life and the chase. Much more ambiguous is the other sculptured altar from London, which was found in Smithfield and is now in the London Museum. (*Fig. 48.*) This is very crudely carved, and al-

Fig. 48 *Limestone altar from Smithfield, with relief of Mercury*

though it presumably represents Mercury—who, as guide of the dead, may have had a small shrine in the Roman cemetery—the native sculptor has produced an image much more like the horned warrior-god of North Britain.[2] The winged hat has become a

[1] Ibid., p. 216.
[2] Ibid., pp. 155–8.

distinct pair of horns, and the caduceus a curious fork-like weapon, which is brandished high in the air. If the figure harks back to the iconography of a native tribal deity, it no less strikingly fore-shadows that of the horned medieval devil with his pitchfork. Anything more remote from the standard representation of a classical god can hardly be imagined.

Small bronze figurines of Mercury, Minerva, Hercules and other Roman deities, said to be from London, can be seen in the London and Guildhall Museums. In many cases, however, their history is suspect, and as they are accompanied in the London collections by small Etruscan and other bronzes of a much earlier period, also alleged to be from the City, their genuineness as London finds must be doubted, especially when they have a fine, hard patina of a kind that is rare in London. Equally dubious are some of the red terra-cotta figures of Italian origin, several of which are much too early to be finds from Londinium.[1] It seems likely that there were London dealers in the nineteenth century who took advantage of collectors' interest in London excavations to find a market for their imported antiquities, which were sold through labourers on City sites, especially those (such as Liverpool Street Station) where genuine finds had stimulated a demand that exceeded the supply. There is no reason, however, to doubt the London provenance of the bronze figurines of Mercury, Apollo and (probably) Jupiter, recovered by Roach Smith from the dredging at London Bridge, and now in the British Museum. (*Fig. 49.*) Small figures of this kind, only a few inches high, were kept in household shrines and were also used for votive purposes. This may explain their presence in the river, but a curious feature is that all were broken, perhaps deliberately, and Roach Smith suggested that this might be the work of Christian iconoclasts.

Fully authenticated also are the pipe-clay figurines of deities, to which reference has already been made. These have been found in archaeological contexts in London, and they are in any case mostly too fragmentary to be collectors' pieces. They were manufactured in moulds in the Allier region of central France and in the neigh-bourhood of Cologne, and found a ready market in Britain. Goddesses were favoured rather than gods, and in London the most popular was Venus, whose figurines outnumber even those of the mother-goddess and are to be found in all the big London collec-

---

[1] E.g. a fine, large terra-cotta figure of a goddess holding a fruit, from Liverpool Street, now in Guildhall Museum, which, according to Mr R. A. Higgins, is of the 4th century BC.

Fig. 49 *Bronze figurines from the Thames at London Bridge*
(a) *Apollo* ($4\frac{1}{2}$ *in.*) (b) *Mercury* ($4\frac{1}{2}$ *in.*)

Fig. 50 *Pipeclay figurine of Venus from London* ($6\frac{3}{4}$ *in.*)

173

tions. (*Fig. 50.*) She is represented naked and braiding her hair, like the classical Venus rising from the sea. The superficial impression is that of an imported Roman deity, whose popularity might suggest that love was one of the principal interests of Londinium. It is clear, however, that the figurines are the manifestation of a Gaulish cult, and the Celtic deity identified with the Mediterranean goddess was probably concerned with general fertility rather than love and beauty. There is also a suggestion from the associations of these figures elsewhere that she may have been a goddess of springs and streams.[1] The type of Venus emerging from the water would of course be quite appropriate for a deity of this kind, and it may be noted that about half of the London figurines whose find-spots are known came from the Walbrook valley. A few of the others came from Roman cemetery areas, and there is evidence of a custom, which cannot easily be explained, of burying such figurines with the dead.[2] These circumstances all suggest that the Gaulish goddess who became so popular in London had much wider interests than the Italian Venus whose form she took.

In addition to the nursing mother-goddess and the Venus figures, there is in Guildhall Museum a portion of a pipe-clay figure from Leadenhall Street, representing Diana as Luna with the crescent moon behind her head. There are also pipe-clay figures of cocks, which were sometimes buried with the dead, and in All Hallows Barking Church is a fragment of the figure of a horse, probably found with other Roman antiquities from the site. All these little statuettes had a religious significance, in which the Gaulish elements seem to predominate over the classical.

It is unnecessary to make too much of this distinction, however, since Roman and Celtic paganism now had very much the same attitude towards religion. The gods had to be placated, and could be persuaded to intervene favourably in human affairs—for a consideration. Under the influence of Roman commercialism, the more primitive conception of sacrifice as a creative act, renewing the life of the deity, had been largely superseded by the idea of a gift to the god as a payment for favours received or awaited. Bargains with the supernatural powers were constantly being made, and the settlement was often the provision of a new altar or cult-figure—debts that numerous inscriptions inform us were 'gladly paid'. Setting up a miniature shrine or purchasing a cheap pipe-clay statuette to place

---

[1] F. Jenkins: 'The Cult of the Pseudo-Venus in Kent', in *Arch. Cant.*, LXXII (1958), pp. 64–6.
[2] Ibid., p. 67. List of London finds, pp. 71–2.

in an established sanctuary was an economical way of doing the same thing, within reach of the poor, and perhaps also regarded by wealthier people as an appropriate lesser payment for minor favours. A beautiful enamelled plaque representing an altar, found in the Thames and now in the British Museum, was evidently intended as a substitute for an actual altar, presumably dedicated to the god of the river. (*Fig. 51*.) This is of high quality, however, and can hardly have been less expensive than a stone altar.

Fig. 51 *Enamelled bronze plaque in form of altar, found in the Thames (7 in.)*

Gifts to the gods could, of course, be of many kinds. The sacrifice of animals and the pouring of libations were among them, and even human sacrifice in the attenuated form of infanticide seems to have lingered on, perhaps surreptitiously, in Kent, where infant burials as foundation deposits have been found at Springhead and Reculver.

175

In London itself there are indications that a strange and very barbarous custom was practised on at least one occasion. In the Walbrook numerous human skulls have been found without bones from the accompanying skeletons, and it seems reasonably certain that they were thrown into the stream as decapitated heads. This evidently followed a massacre, and it has been plausibly suggested that the occasion was the capture of Londinium by Boudicca. If so, it seems likely that this was not an act of mere terrorism, but had a religious significance. Before they were civilized by the Romans, the Celtic peoples were head-hunters who, like their modern counterparts in South-East Asia, regarded the heads which they took not as mere trophies, but as objects of supernatural power to be venerated. As such, they might be dedicated to the gods, and in Celtic myth and custom they have a specially close association with sacred waters. There are a number of indications suggesting that the local deity who was the special patron of Londinium was the water spirit who lived in the Walbrook, and on one occasion at least he (or she) seems to have received an appropriate sacrifice of human heads. It is possible that a human skull deposited in the well in Queen Street where the 'bikini' trunks were found (*p. 153*) had a similar significance. This was thrown in after the well had silted up and was pushed down with a heavy piece of wood. There would be no reason to regard it as anything but a rather curious piece of refuse if there were not numerous other finds of skulls in Romano-British wells, and also many Celtic legends about the magical power of heads in wells.[1] In this case, the lower jaw was missing, and it seems to have been the skull of someone long dead rather than a recently decapitated head which was thrown in. Fresh heads were presumably less easy to obtain in the Flavian period when this event occurred, but a skull may have been considered equally effective.

Dogs seem to have been regarded as appropriate sacrifices, especially to deities of the underworld; and this may explain the burial of two dogs with Roman pottery in a box-like structure, apparently not a well, found a few years ago under Newington Causeway at the Elephant and Castle. It may also account for the cremated remains of two dogs in a shaft near the mausoleum at Keston.[2]

Offerings to the gods could also be personal possessions of many

---

[1] Anne Ross: op. cit., pp. 104–13.
[2] *Arch. Cant.*, LXXVIII (1963), pp. l–li.

kinds, and there is a strong suspicion that some at least of the tools and ornaments found in such abundance in the Walbrook were deliberately deposited there for this purpose. It is difficult to account in any other way for the failure to retrieve so many large tools from such a small stream. Coins, also, were considered acceptable, and these likewise abound in the Walbrook.

Offerings of coins were also made as a substitute for a foundation sacrifice—a custom to which reference has already been made in connexion with the Roman bridge. (*See pp. 25 ff.*) In Guildhall Museum is shown a handful of unofficial coins of the late third century, which were deliberately buried on the site of Lloyd's in Lime Street in the interval between the demolition of a house and the building of its successor. Since the coins were at foundation-level and would have been inaccessible after the floor was laid, it seems likely that their purpose was to bring luck to the new house.[1] A single copper coin (*as*) of Antoninus Pius in a pot buried in the make-up beneath the floor of a building in King's Head Yard, Southwark,[2] was probably put there for the same reason. A large coin (*sestertius*) of Postumus found in the chalk puddling at the bottom of a well on the site of St Swithin's House, Walbrook, also seems to have been a votive offering deposited when the well was constructed. The coin found in the mast-step of the Blackfriars barge, shown in Guildhall Museum, was evidently the nautical equivalent of a foundation deposit, and in this case Fortuna, the goddess of luck, was further flattered by the selection of a coin that bore her effigy. (*See p. 38.*)

Misfortunes were also averted by means of amulets that were believed to have a magical power of their own, independent of the favour of the gods. Representations of the male organ, in particular, seem to have been regarded almost as lightning conductors, capable of diverting harmlessly to themselves the malign influence of the evil eye. Bronze phalli with loops for suspension and a carving of male genitalia on a piece of antler, perforated so that it could be worn, can be seen in Guildhall Museum, where there is also a little gold ring for a small child, with the same emblem. The last example demonstrates very clearly that the purpose of the amulet was neither to arouse desire nor to bestow fertility, but was purely protective. The representation of a clenched fist with thumb

---

[1] The circumstances of the deposit are described in detail in *Numismatic Chronicle*, 6th ser., XV, pp. 113–24.
[2] K. M. Kenyon: *Excavations in Southwark*, 1959, p. 21.

protruding between the fingers was another symbol of the same thing, and had the same magical significance. The belief in the evil influence that can be exerted, even unconsciously, by the glance of envy remains strong in southern Italy today, and phallic amulets and gestures are still used to combat it.

There was, however, a darker side to the superstition of Roman London, and two examples of a malevolent practice can be seen— one in the London Museum and the other in the British Museum. These are curses scratched on sheet lead, which were subsequently nailed to structures of some kind, probably wooden shrines on the banks of the Walbrook, since they were both found near the stream. The first, which was fixed with a single nail, and has its edges slightly melted by heat, comes from the site of the National Provincial Bank in Prince's Street. On both sides is scratched practically the same inscription:

T. EGNATIVS TYRANVS DEFIC(T)VS EST ET P. CICEREIVS FELIX DEFICTVS EST (the last two words being omitted as understood on one side).

It means:
'Titus Egnatius Tyranus is cursed and Publius Cicereius Felix is cursed'.

The British Museum curse, which was found in Telegraph Street, east of Moorgate Street, is much more elaborate and was determinedly fixed with seven nails—a magical number—driven from a side that was uninscribed, so that the inscription could not be read when it was fixed in position. (*Fig. 52.*) It has been translated as follows:

'I curse Tretia Maria and her life and mind and memory and liver and lungs mixed up together, and her words, thoughts and memory; thus may she be unable to speak what things are concealed, nor be able . . . . . . nor . . . . '[1]

The phrasing of this particularly virulent curse suggests either that the intended victim was a blackmailer, or that she had discovered an important secret, which could only be safeguarded by destroying

[1] *RIB,* 7.

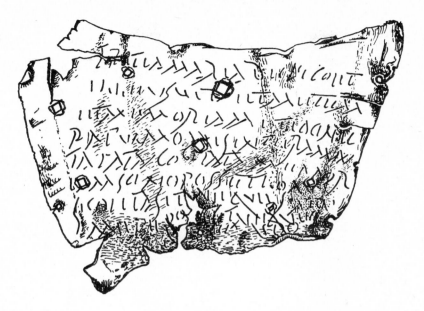

Fig. 52 *Lead 'curse' from Telegraph Street*

her. No god is invoked by name on either of these curses, but they were presumably intended to work through the influence of a deity, perhaps one of the dark powers of the underworld.

There was little to satisfy the spiritual needs of man in all this arid paganism, which reduced religion to the level of a cold commercial transaction. In particular, there was nothing to give comfort to those facing death or suffering bereavement. The souls of the dead went to a shadowy half-existence in the underworld, and the principal object of the funeral rites seems to have been to dispatch them on their dismal journey, for which they were provided with food, drink, toilet equipment and so on, as for earthly travel. The containers for these commodities are found buried with the cremation urns, and this is the source of most of the complete pots in the museum collections. On occasion the mourners seem to have tried to ensure that the journey was one-way only—as for example in a burial recently found at the Old Bailey. The cremation was in a large, globular amphora, the single opening of which was covered

179

with a vertical tile, against which three pottery lids had been set, as if to reinforce the closing of the entrance with a ritual barrier.

The purpose of small pipe-clay figurines occasionally buried with the dead is not clear. Some were perhaps offerings to underworld deities, since they are also found in shrines; and some may have been merely toys buried with children. It has been suggested that the rather rare busts of boys, an example of which from the Liverpool Street cemetery can be seen in Guildhall Museum, were substitutes for the *imago* or effigy of the deceased.[1] A similar figure in the London Museum, however, was found in the Walbrook area in Copthall Court, and is more likely to have come from the stream itself or one of the small public shrines on its banks than from a domestic *lararium*, where effigies of the family dead might be expected.

A spiritual malaise seems to have been general in the Roman world in the latter days of paganism, perhaps partly because the *Pax Romana* and the more efficient organization of life gave men more leisure to contemplate their own mortality. Not unnaturally they looked for kindlier gods and a glimmer of hope, both of which were to be found in the religions of the east. Roman conquests had opened new channels of communication and the spiritual tide moved strongly from east to west. Juvenal complained that the Orontes, the Nile and the Halys flowed into the Tiber; they also reached the Thames. The eastern religions came to the west as mystery cults, whose worshippers had to undergo initiation and thereafter were bound by oaths of secrecy. In return they received the warmth of a great emotional experience, and above all were given hope. For these diverse cults had one thing in common: they promised their initiates a full and happy life after death.

It was probably due to the influx of ideas from the east, and the new attitude towards the after-life, that a great change took place in burial customs. The two practices of cremation and the inhumation of the unburnt body were both of great antiquity, and to some extent co-existed throughout the Roman period. Cremation, however, was the general rule in early times, and later was almost completely superseded by inhumation. Christian views on the resurrection of the body no doubt played an important part in effecting this change, and eventually made it practically complete, but the spread of inhumation was much more rapid than that of

[1] J. M. C. Toynbee: *Art in Roman Britain*, 1964, p. 423.

Fig. 53 *Pottery jug from Southwark with scratched inscription* LONDINI AD FANVM ISIDIS: *'At London, at the Temple of Isis'*

Christianity, and older ideas from Egypt and Western Asia certainly contributed to the same trend. The great period of change in Italy itself was the second century but, as might be expected, the full effect was not felt in the far west until a little later, and it was in the third century that inhumation generally replaced cremation in Britain.

The cult of the Egyptian goddess Isis was early established beside the Thames, as is attested by the wine-jug with the *graffito* referring to her shrine in London, found in Tooley Street and now in the London Museum. (*See p. 141.*) Fragments of similar jugs were found in a mid-second-century deposit at King's Head Yard,[1] Southwark, but this also included a fair amount of first-century material, and the type is usually regarded as Flavian. (*Fig. 53.*)

Isis is also represented in the London Museum by a bronze bust

[1] K. M. Kenyon: op. cit., p. 71, no. 22.

Fig. 54 *Silver figure of Horus (Harpocrates) with gold chain, from the Thames at London Bridge (3 in.)*

wearing a lotus head-dress, but this was a steelyard weight, almost certainly imported, and it does not necessarily have any connexion with her cult in London. A similar bust held in a hand,[1] forming the ornamental head of a bone hair-pin from Moorgate in the same collection, testifies only to the popularity of the goddess among some ladies. A magnificent marble head of her husband Serapis-Osiris was found in the Walbrook Mithraeum, as we shall see, but here he had been assimilated into Mithraic worship by that process of syncretism which was a characteristic feature of late Roman paganism. Harpocrates or Horus, son of Isis and Osiris, is represented by two votive or cult figurines in the British Museum. One of these is a charming little silver figure with a gold chain knotted round it, found in the Thames at London Bridge. (*Fig. 54.*) The

[1] Incorrectly described as Cybele in *London in R. Times*, p. 103, as was pointed out by E. & J. Harris: *The Oriental Cults in Roman Britain*, 1965, p. 80.

god is represented as a winged Cupid, with a dog, tortoise and bird at his feet, but is recognizable as Harpocrates by the characteristic position of his right hand, which points to his lips in a gesture enjoining secrecy—a reminder that the sacred mysteries of Isis were not to be divulged to the uninitiated. The other, from an unknown locality in London, is of bronze, and shows the god wearing the double crown of Egypt, with his right hand raised in the same gesture, while the left holds a cornucopiae. A terra-cotta bust of a chubby boy wearing a lunar pendant, found in Great Winchester Street and now in Guildhall Museum, may also represent this deity.

The cult of Cybele, the Great Mother-Goddess of Asia Minor, was also almost certainly introduced into London, although there is an element of doubt about most of the finds that are attributed to it. A limestone figure of a youth wearing a Phrygian cap and holding a bow, in the British Museum collection, is usually regarded as Attis, the lover of Cybele, a god of vegetation who was believed to die and be resurrected each year. It was found in Bevis Marks, and may well have come originally from a sepulchral monument, perhaps incorporated later in a bastion of the wall. A bronze figure from the Thames at London Bridge, wearing a similar cap and holding clusters of fruit, also represents Attis.[1] It has been suggested that a limestone figure from Drury Lane in the London Museum is likely to be Attis, holding a shepherd's curved stick, rather than Cautopates, the torch-bearing companion of Mithras, as was formerly thought.[2] If so, it may have come from a sepulchral monument over a grave. It is doubtful, however, whether it originally stood in the neighbourhood where it was found, and it may be significant that a marble tombstone with a Greek inscription, almost certainly an import of recent centuries, also comes from Drury Lane. The goddess herself is represented by a terra-cotta head with turreted crown in Guildhall Museum. This is said to have been found in Paul Street, Finsbury, but there is considerable doubt about it as a find of Roman London, since it has been identified by the British Museum as Greek of the second century BC.

The cult of Cybele was an orgiastic religion with unpleasant and even barbaric aspects, with which a curious bronze object in the British Museum, from the Thames at London Bridge, may be connected. (*Fig. 55.*) This superficially resembles a pair of nut-crackers and seems to be a sort of clamp used to exert considerable

[1] *IRL*, p. 69, Pl. XIX.
[2] J. M. C. Toynbee: *Art in Britain under the Romans*, 1964, p. 93.

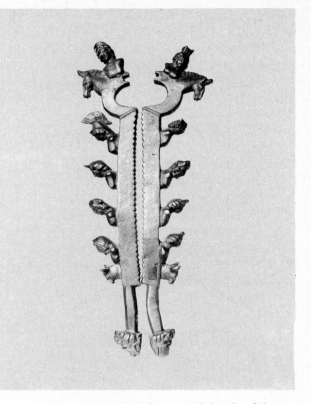

Fig. 55 *Bronze clamp with heads of deities,*
probably used in cult of Cybele, from the
Thames at London Bridge (11 in.)

pressure. It is decorated with busts of the Roman deities of the days
of the week (Saturn, Sol, Luna, Mars, Mercury, Jupiter, Venus and
Fortuna) on the sides, and with two other busts, thought to be of
Attis and Cybele, above horses' heads at the top. It seems to be a
ritual implement of some kind and, if the two most prominent busts
are correctly identified, is likely to be connected with the cult of
Cybele. The suggestion has been made that it was used in the
castration of the priests of the goddess,[1] or else that it was a curb
fitted over the nose of the bull to control it in the *taurobolium*, a
sacrifice in which the initiates washed in the blood of the bull.[2]

A frog moulded in relief on a piece of pottery from the Walbrook
stream near the Mithraeum, in Guildhall Museum, is probably

[1] A. G. Francis: *Proceedings of the Royal Society of Medicine*, XIX (1926), pp. 95 ff.
[2] E. & J. Harris: op. cit., p. 112.

from a pot decorated also with snakes and lizards—a type of vessel associated with the cult of Sabazios, a Phrygian mystery god, sometimes identified with Zeus, sometimes with Dionysus, and closely akin to Attis as a god of vegetation and wild life.[1]

The greatest of all the pagan mystery religions, however, was that of Mithras, originally a Persian god of light, whose worship came to the Roman world by way of Asia Minor, where the god acquired his characteristic head-dress, the Phrygian cap. His cult, which was organized as a closely-knit secret society for men only, became especially popular among merchants and soldiers, by whom it was carried to all the great ports and the farthest frontiers of the Roman world. Most of the eastern mystery religions laid their greatest stress on the act of initiation as a means of salvation, and were concerned only exceptionally with imposing a code of conduct in life. Mithraism, however, retained the high ideals of the Persian religion from which it sprang, and was firmly on the side of good in the great struggle of the universe. With its insistence on honesty, purity and courage, it was a religion well suited to men of affairs who could appreciate the need for these virtues, but lacked the austere temperament necessary to achieve them, like a Marcus Aurelius, by standing alone on the bleak heights of Stoic philosophy. The strongest appeal of Mithraism was not to the poor and dispossessed, like Christianity, or to the emotionally unstable, like the cult of Cybele, but to men who were actively engaged in the business of the Empire as officials, soldiers and traders—classes strongly represented in London. It would be surprising if the small but wealthy Mithraeum on the east bank of the Walbrook were the only one in the city, although we have as yet no evidence of any other.

The actual building, which was apparently constructed towards the end of the second century, has already been described (*pp. 92–5*), so it will suffice to draw attention to its remarkable similarity to an early Christian church. Architecturally they are closely akin, since both served the same purpose of housing a congregation for worship and for communion with the deity—quite unlike the older type of pagan temple, which was merely a shrine for the god, whose worshippers stood outside. In two respects only were there minor differences: in the earlier phases the side aisles of the Mithraeum were raised wooden benches on which the congregation sat at a slightly higher level than the central nave, and there was a shallow

---

[1] J. M. C. Toynbee: *Art in Britain under the Romans*, 1964, p. 395.

well or water-tank at the western end of the south aisle. It seemed at first that this basilican building might prove to be a Christian church, since even the orientation was the same as that of the early churches—i.e. east–west, with the sanctuary to the west. (The transfer of the Christian sanctuary to the eastern end of the church came later, as a result of liturgical changes.) The orientation of the Mithraeum clearly has reference to the course of the sun, for the sun-god was an ally of Mithras, and was sometimes practically identified with him. A fragment of a dedicatory inscription from the temple refers to the 'unconquered sun-god' and also to the course of the sun, *ab oriente ad occidentem.*

The true nature of the building was revealed by the discovery of the first of the fine marble sculptures. (*Fig. 56.*) This was at once

Fig. 56 *Marble head of Mithras from the Walbrook Mithraeum (height 14½ in.)*

recognized as the head of Mithras, by the Phrygian cap and by the slightly averted angle of the head, which is the characteristic attitude of the god when sacrificing the great bull—the central mystery of the Mithraic legend. The story is that, before the creation of earthly life, Mithras, who although divine was not the supreme God, was ordered to capture and kill the primeval bull. After various adventures he dragged it to a cave and stabbed it, with his face averted in pity. From the blood and semen of the bull, shed in this single sacrifice, came all the useful life on the earth, in spite of the opposition of the powers of evil and death.

Like the other marble sculptures found in the temple, the head of Mithras is of Italian marble, and was imported as a finished work of art, probably made to order at the time the Mithraeum was built. The head is somewhat flattened behind, and probably formed part of a bull-slaying group that stood in the central alcove of the sanctuary. Since no trace of the rest of the group was found, it seems likely that it was made merely of stucco, and was left to its fate when the valuable head was removed.

Other finds followed in quick succession: first, a female head of greyish marble, on the crown of which a head-dress, presumably of different material, had originally been fixed. This was almost certainly a metal helmet, and there is little doubt that the sculpture represents Minerva. Then, within a foot or so of the earlier finds, three more marble sculptures were found together: a little figure of Mercury, represented with a ram (as a pastoral god), a tortoise beneath his left foot (as the inventor of the lyre, which he made from a tortoise's shell) and holding in his left hand a purse (as the patron of travellers and merchants); a great hand gripping the hilt of a dagger, and evidently representing the sacrificial hand of Mithras; and, finest of all, the bearded head of Serapis wearing a corn-measure decorated with olive-branches. (*Fig. 57.*)

The hand of Mithras is in an appropriate context, but is puzzling because of its size, since a bull-slaying group on this scale could not have been accommodated in such a small building. It certainly did not stand outside, for the surface of the marble is quite unweathered, and in any case the cult image of a mystery religion would not have been displayed in a public place. The idea of a Mithraic 'cathedral' elsewhere in London is so wildly improbable that it can be disregarded; and it must therefore be assumed that the hand never formed part of a group, but was shown by itself as a symbol of the great sacrifice. An iron shank projecting from the base of the hand

Fig. 57 *Marble head of Serapis from the Walbrook Mithraeum (height 12¾ in.)*

was evidently used to attach it, and it is likely that there was a representation of the sleeve to mask the junction with the surface to which it was fixed.

The presence of the other deities in a Mithraeum is not really surprising, since the later paganism was moving towards monotheism and tended to regard the various gods and goddesses as different manifestations of the same divinity. Moreover, the deities represented by the sculptures have one important thing in common: they are all concerned in some way with the after-life: Minerva as the conqueror of death, Mercury as the guide of the dead on their last journey, and Serapis as the master of everything beneath the surface of the earth, and therefore the lord of the dead in the Underworld.

The condition of these long-buried sculptures is remarkable. Mercury had been broken and repaired in Roman times, and the right hand holding the caduceus is missing, as was evidently the case when the figure was buried. The head of Mithras, when found, had suffered some staining from an iron incrustation containing a carbon deposit, perhaps the result of exposure to the altar fires,[1] and was in two pieces, but is otherwise undamaged. The heads of Serapis and Minerva (apart from the missing helmet) and the great hand are practically perfect. Both of these heads retain their original highly-polished surfaces, and Serapis, in particular, must still look very much as he did when he left the sculptor's workshop in Italy almost eighteen centuries ago. Yet he is heavy and fragile, and would suffer grave damage from a fall of a few inches. It is clear that these sculptures were very carefully laid where they were found, and equally carefully covered with earth. The stratification showed that this took place after the seven pairs of columns, probably symbolizing the seven grades of initiation, had been removed, so that the building had become an open hall, with only a slight difference in level between nave and aisles. It evidently continued in use, since at least two more floors were laid after the burial of the sculptures. Professor Grimes's final assessment of the dating evidence has not yet been published, but it would appear, from the coins associated with these later floors, that the marbles were laid in their resting-place very early in the reign of Constantine I. The Mithraea on Hadrian's Wall were destroyed early in the fourth century, and

---

[1] H. J. Plenderleith: *The Conservation of Antiquities and Works of Art: Treatment, Repair and Restoration*, 1956, pp. 312–13. The altar-fuel would have been pine-cones, several of which were found in the Mithraeum. An example is shown in Guildhall Museum.

danger evidently threatened the Walbrook temple. There is little doubt that the sculptures were buried by the Mithraists to save them from destruction, and it seems most likely that the threat came from the Christians, who were more hostile to Mithraism than to any other pagan cult. This was partly because it was the strongest rival of Christianity, and partly because some features of Mithraic ritual —such as baptism by water and a communion meal—were remarkably like Christian practices and seemed like a blasphemous parody of them. The persecution of Mithraists by Christians was general in the reign of Constantine's successors, but it is surprising that Christianity should have been sufficiently powerful to menace the London Mithraeum at the date when the sculptures seem to have been buried. According to tradition, Constantine's mother was a Christian, and his father, Constantius Chlorus, is said to have had some sympathies in this direction; so it may be that Constantine, who was proclaimed Emperor by the army in Britain when his father died at York in 306, was more fully committed to Christianity from the beginning of his reign than it was prudent for him to show elsewhere, until he was in a much stronger position.

The fate of the less choice sculptures that remained unconcealed can be seen from the fragments found in and near the temple: a hand gripping the nostrils of the bull from a small bull-slaying group: the lower part of a relief of Cautopates, the bearer of the inverted torch that symbolized darkness and death: and a broken relief with a portion of one of the Dioscuri, standing beside his horse. These are all of oolitic limestone, and were almost certainly carved in Britain. Since it was impossible to conceal every sculpture in the temple, preference was evidently given to the more valuable works of art in fine Italian marble, and the rest were abandoned to the iconoclasts. There are, however, two male torsos in imported marble, which have been broken in very much the same way, presumably deliberately. These can all be seen in Guildhall Museum, which also contains all the other finds from Professor Grimes's excavation and a scale-model of the Mithraeum itself as it was found. (Casts of the fine marble sculptures are shown in the London Museum and also in a show-case in the entrance hall of Bucklersbury House, very near the spot where they were found.)

There are, however, three sculptures of imported marble, which the London Museum acquired many years ago, with the information that they were found in Walbrook near Bond Court in 1889, and these are exhibited in Kensington Palace. Their genuineness as finds of

Roman London was long in doubt, since the precise circumstances of their discovery were veiled in the mystery that must always surround an illegal transaction. They were first acquired by a dealer from the workmen who found them, and who had, of course, no right of possession. As a safeguard against claims from the legal owner, the freeholder of the site from which they came, the dealer could not be entirely frank about the find-spot, when in due course he sold the sculptures to an antiquary named Ransom, from whose collection they eventually passed to the London Museum. The problem was how far he had departed from the strict truth in saying that they had been found 'in the middle of the Walbrook at a depth of about twenty feet'. They were of Italian marble, and might easily have been brought to Britain in some collection of the Grand Tour, especially as nothing comparable had ever been found in an authentic context of Roman London. Had the 'Walbrook' label been attached to them simply to make them more interesting and therefore add to their value? The discovery of similar sculptures of the same date (middle to late second century) in an archaeological excavation in Walbrook went a long way towards the vindication of the truth of the original story; the fact that these were found at approximately the depth reported for the earlier finds, and immediately adjacent to the foundation of an office built in the late nineteenth century, seems to leave no reasonable doubt that the sculptures in the London Museum did in fact come from the Mithraeum.

One of them is actually a relief of Mithras killing the bull, accompanied by his torch-bearing companions, Cautes and Cautopates, all within a circular frame on which are the signs of the Zodiac—a reminder of the importance of astrology in Mithraism. (*Fig. 58.*) In the upper corners are representations of the sun-god and moon-goddess in their chariots, and in the lower are two heads, probably symbolizing the winds. The sculptured slab was dedicated in fulfilment of a vow by Ulpius Silvanus, a veteran of the Second Legion Augusta, the only member of the congregation of the Mithraeum whose name we know. The inscription also includes the mysterious words: *factus Arausione*— literally 'made at Orange' (Southern Gaul). It is generally agreed that *factus* is applied, not to the relief, but to Silvanus himself, and it could mean either 'enlisted as a soldier', or, used in a technical (Mithraic) sense, 'initiated' in some grade of the society. The carving is believed by Miss J. M. C. Toynbee to be provincial, although the marble itself comes from Italy, and she has pointed out that the closest parallels in

Fig. 58 *Marble relief of Mithras killing the bull, found in Walbrook, 1889 (height 17½ in.)*

composition are from Germany and Pannonia.[1]

There is also the head and chest of a reclining river-god, with a portion of a water plant, probably held in the missing right hand, against his right shoulder. This is of purely classical style, and was certainly carved in Italy. If made to order for the London Mithraeum, as is possible (although Miss Toynbee believes it to be of slightly earlier date[2]) it could partly symbolize the Thames or Walbrook, but certainly also had a wider and more mystical significance—perhaps both as the river separating the dead from the living and as the source of life in this world and the next. Although it is an incomplete figure, it is possible that the piece of marble itself suffered damage only to the arms, and it may be that the lower part was of inferior material, which was abandoned when the upper portion was buried. The damage is of a kind not likely

[1] J. M. C. Toynbee: *Art in Britain under the Romans,* 1964, p. 170.
[2] J. M. C. Toynbee: *Art in Roman Britain,* 1962, p. 138.

to have been inflicted by iconoclasts, who would almost certainly have smashed the face, and is more likely to have been accidental, probably incurred when the figure was found. It seems likely, therefore, that it was deliberately concealed with the complete bull-slaying relief and with the sculptures already described that were found in 1954.

The third figure in the London Museum is headless, but otherwise is only slightly damaged, and it seems likely that it was buried as an almost complete sculpture like the others, and suffered its worst injuries when it was found by workmen. There are two possibilities that might account for the complete absence of the head: that it was wholly shattered, probably by a pick, or that it was sold with the rest of the sculptures, but passed into other hands as a souvenir of convenient size. The figure represents a Genius, probably the Genius of London, as a ship's prow in waves is shown beside him. He holds a cornucopiae in the left hand, and with the right makes an offering with a patera at an altar, from which a snake rises and twines round his right wrist. This sculpture also is in classical style and would have been carved in Italy.

The Mithraists who buried all these fine works of art no doubt hoped that better times would come, when they could be restored to places of honour. Evidently this did not happen, as they remained buried and were eventually forgotten. This raises the problem of the subsequent use of the building, since it was not destroyed and two more floors were laid after the sculptures were buried. There is no indication at all that it ever became a Christian church; on the contrary, there is clear evidence that paganism did return, and as the last structural alteration was the setting up of a stone altar-base in the apse, it must be assumed that the building was still a place of worship.[1] The date of this was about or after the middle of the reign of Constantine I, as was shown by coins found beneath the altar-slab, but seems unlikely to be as late as the revival of paganism under the Emperor Julian.

In the final phase, a marble group representing Bacchus, the wine-god, with his retinue, lay in the north-east corner of the building, where it seems to have remained unmolested as the temple fell into ruins. (*Fig. 59.*) This can now be seen in Guildhall Museum. The god stands beside a tree on which a vine has been trained, with his hand holding a snake, which is twined round a branch. He is

---

[1] W. F. Grimes, in R. L. S. Bruce-Mitford (ed.): *Recent Archaeological Excavations in Britain*, 1956, p. 141.

Fig. 59 *Marble group of Bacchus, with Silenus,*
satyr, maenad and panther,
from the Walbrook Mithraeum (height 13½ in.)

accompanied by a satyr, a maenad holding the mysterious box used in his secret rites, a panther, and Silenus holding a wine-cup while riding on an ass. Up in the tree is a small figure of the goat-legged Pan with the upper portion unfortunately missing, as are the heads of the satyr and maenad. On the base is a roughly carved inscription, HOMINIBVS BAGIS BITAM, in which the last two B's have replaced V's, as was not uncommon in late Latin. It should therefore be read HOMINIBVS VAGIS VITAM—'(*Give*) *life to wandering men*'. The wine-god is evidently shown here in his role of a saviour-god, who confers immortality on his initiates. This was of course quite a different mystery cult from that of Mithras, and it may be that in its final phases the Walbrook temple was not a Mithraeum. There was, however, a strong tendency for the pagan cults to coalesce in the later stages of their struggle with Christianity, so the presence of Bacchus does not necessarily imply the departure of Mithras. It may incidentally be noted that the two marble torsos, to which reference has already been made, are very similar to the torso of Bacchus as represented here, and may also come from figures of this god.

The Bacchic group is of imported marble, probably Italian, but is provincial in style, and Miss Toynbee has suggested that it may be of Balkan origin.[1] She believes that it dates from about the middle of the third century, and if this view is correct, it was presumably brought to the Walbrook temple a considerable time after it was made. There is no indication of deliberate damage in antiquity, and its worst injuries seem to have been inflicted when it was found, unfortunately by contractor's workmen, in a part of the site that Professor Grimes had not excavated. The upper portion of Pan, the head of the snake, the left hand of Bacchus, and the heads of the satyr and maenad have all been detached by modern breaks, and were nowhere to be found when this area was thoroughly searched by archaeologists a short time after the discovery.

It is curious that in several instances there is a strong suggestion that influences reached the London Mithraeum from the Danubian provinces, and this may well indicate that influential members of the congregation themselves came from those parts. The most striking of these affinities with Eastern Europe is to be seen in a broken marble roundel in Guildhall Museum. (*Fig. 60.*) This represents in low relief two rider-gods, the Thracian counterparts

---

[1] J. M. C. Toynbee: *Art in Britain under the Romans*, 1964, pp. 69–70.

Fig. 60 *Marble medallion representing twin Danubian rider-gods and goddess, from the Walbrook Mithraeum (diameter 4⅜ in.)*

of the Dioscuri, on either side of a goddess, with a fish on a table in front of her. It has been suggested that she is the equivalent of Atargatis, the Syrian nature-goddess[1], but she is undoubtedly represented here as the central figure of a distinctively Danubian mystery cult. There is a human body lying beneath one rider and a snake beneath the other, while in the exergue of the medallion are a dog, a vase and a bird. Similar medallions, most commonly in lead, have been found in a concentration centring on the Middle Danube, and are very rare in the west.[2] The London roundel was found in one of the later levels of the temple, and is tentatively attributed by Miss Toynbee to the third century.[3]

The Walbrook Mithraeum reserved its most dramatic find until the very end of Professor Grimes's investigation. Just before the destruction of the building commenced, he persuaded the contractors to remove a nineteenth-century foundation block that had been set

[1] Ibid., pp. 167–8.
[2] *Jahrbuch des Römisch-Germanischen Zentralmuseums*, Mainz, V (1958), pp. 259 ff.
[3] J. M. C. Toynbee: *Art in Britain under the Romans*, 1964, p. 168.

into the north wall, and so was able to get an unimpeded view of the whole structure for photography. During the process of cleaning up before the photograph was taken, anything that looked as if it might be of any interest was put in a bag labelled 'from disturbed level above north wall' and sent to Guildhall Museum. In addition to a number of scraps of pottery and metal, the bag contained a curious cylindrical object, covered with a thick, black deposit and quite unrecognizable; it could, of course, have been of any date up to the late nineteenth century. This has since proved to be one of the most interesting objects in Guildhall Museum—so precious that under present circumstances it is possible only to exhibit an electro-type replica of it.

It was noticed that there appeared to be a trace of decoration under the black deposit, and the object was sent to the London Museum for skilful cleaning. It proved to be of high-quality silver, originally gilt, and was covered with strange figures of animals and men in late Roman style. (*Fig. 61.*) It was a box about $2\frac{1}{2}$ in. high and 3 in. in diameter, with a hinged lid, and inside was another cylindrical silver object, with a pattern of small holes in the bottom and the top closed only by a trifid bar. A Coroner's Inquest was held

Fig. 61 *Silver box and strainer from the Walbrook Mithraeum (height of container $2\frac{1}{2}$ in.)*

on the find, and it was declared to be Treasure Trove, since the only possible explanation of its survival seemed to be that it had been deliberately concealed in a secret place in the wall, immediately beneath the nineteenth-century foundation.[1]

There can be no doubt that the object in the decorated casket was used in the ritual of the temple, but how? It has been described as a sprinkler or strainer, but the trifid 'handle', though suitable for suspension, does not provide a practical hold for sprinkling; and the holes seem too small for it to have been used for straining honey, as was suggested by Miss Toynbee[2]—or indeed any liquid thicker than water. The trifid bar can be closely paralleled in Roman corn-measures, where it had the very practical purpose of preventing cramming and ensuring that precisely the same amount went into the measure each time. If it had the same purpose here, the contents must have consisted of solid particles larger than the holes, and the object can only have been used as an infuser. Is it in fact a druggist's infuser, intended to contain a measured dose of some herbal preparation, which had to be soaked in a certain volume of water to produce a drug of known efficacy? We have no evidence that Mithraists used drugs, but it seems quite likely that they did, if only to induce an apparent 'death' that preceded the initiate's 'rebirth' into the Mithraic community. It is of interest, in view of the Danubian affinities of other finds, to note that the only similar strainer was found in a third-century grave in Strážě, Slovakia.[3] The box seems to have been merely a casket for the strainer, perhaps not originally made for it, and would not have been the container in which an infusion was produced. There were, however, a number of silver fragments found at the same time as the box and strainer, and these form part of the rim and upper portion of a silver bowl. Was this perhaps the container for the liquid, concealed in the same place, probably inverted over the casket, and destroyed when the nineteenth-century foundation was laid?

The decorated casket deserves close examination, for the scenes on it portray a very strange world indeed, and nobody has yet produced a satisfactory explanation of them. In my view they do

[1] Treasure Trove must consist of gold or silver, the owner of which is unknown, deliberately concealed with a view to recovery. Since the City has Charter rights to Treasure Trove found within its limits, the box and contents were successfully claimed for Guildhall Museum. Professor Grimes received a reward of its full value, in accordance with the usual practice, and gave the whole sum to the excavation fund.

[2] J. M. C. Toynbee: *A Silver Casket and Strainer from the Walbrook Mithraeum in the City of London*, Leiden, 1963, p. 8.

[3] Ibid., p. 8 and pl. XII.

not represent a hunt, with some reference to Mithras as a hunter of evil, as has been suggested.[1] Some are certainly scenes of conflict and confrontation, not only between men and animals, but also between various animals, and if they recall any aspect of daily life, it is in the arena rather than the hunting field. Underlying them might easily be Mithraic symbolism of the universal struggle, although specialists in such matters are unable to recognize here anything specifically connected with Mithraism. The box was probably made in the late third or fourth century, so could have been in use either in the earlier, definitely Mithraic, phase of the temple, being concealed when the sculptures were buried, or in the later phase of which we know so little.

The most interesting scenes, however, show griffins carrying coffin-like boxes, which they are trying to open, and men being helped by other men out of boxes, one of which seems to be on wheels. (*Fig. 62.*) Now there is a close parallel to the scene with the

Fig. 62 *Lid of silver box from the Walbrook Mithraeum, showing griffins with boxes, and a man emerging from a box (diameter* $3\frac{1}{8}$ *in.)*

[1] Ibid., pp. 14–15.

griffins at the far end of a fine fourth-century mosaic, in the palatial residence at Piazza Armerina in Sicily. In this case the rest of the scenes do in fact show a series of hunts of a special kind: the animals are being trapped alive and taken on board ship, presumably for use in the arena. The fierce griffin in the last scene of the sequence has his claws in a crate similar to those used to transport the animals, and between its bars can be seen the pale face of a man. It has been suggested that the griffin is about to be caught by a trap containing human bait, but there is no obvious mechanism by which this could be achieved, and the griffin appears to be as much in control of the situation as the men are elsewhere. Surely this is a case of 'the biter bit', and the message is that as a man captures wild animals and carries them off, so in turn he will be carried off himself. The use of a griffin as a symbol of death would not be surprising, as they are commonly represented as guardians of tombs.

From the evidence of the mosaic it can be assumed that in the scenes on the lid of the Walbrook casket, the two boxes that are being attacked by griffins contain men—and here again there is no suggestion at all that the griffins are about to be trapped. The actual capture would have been a much more dramatic moment, which would surely have been depicted in at least one of these three scenes, if the idea had been in the artist's mind. It is much more likely that these are emblems of death, which in the context of a mystery cult was the threshold of a new life. It may be that the men emerging from other boxes represent this resurrection, perhaps as it was enacted in an initiation ceremony. Such symbolism would be most appropriate on the container of an infuser used in that very ritual; it all fits very neatly—and may, of course, be quite wrong!

The rich legacy left by a pagan mystery cult contrasts ironically with the almost complete absence of visible evidence from Roman London of the religion that vanquished it. For more than a hundred years antiquaries have searched eagerly for signs of Christianity in Londinium, but when the various misinterpretations and post-Roman imports have been eliminated, practically nothing remains but a *Chi-Rho* monogram (the first two Greek letters of the name of Christ) roughly scratched on the base of a pewter bowl from Copthall Court in the London Museum. (*Fig. 63.*) This Christian symbol also occurs stamped on eight ingots of pewter, found in the Thames near Battersea Bridge, six of which are in the British Museum. The *Chi-Rho* is accompanied in these stamps either by the words SPES IN DEO ('hope in God') or by the letters *alpha*

Fig. 63 Chi-Rho *monogram on base of pewter bowl from Copthall Court*

and *omega*, the first and last letters of the Greek alphabet, used as a symbol of God. There is also the name SYAGRIUS or SYAGRI stamped on these ingots, however, and this raises a strong suspicion that they have nothing to do with Roman London, but are among the very few objects from the London area that can be attributed to the Dark Ages following the abandonment of Britain by Honorius. For Syagrius was the name of the Roman ruler of North Gaul who was overthrown by Clovis, King of the Franks, in 486, and it seems likely that these official-looking stamps would have been used by the authority of such a ruler, rather than of some person unknown to history who happened to have the same name.[1]

[1] I am indebted to Mr M. Henig for this suggestion.

We have never found any of the churches of Roman London, and have no idea whether any existing City church originated in Roman times. Certainly no indication of this has been found on any church site that has been excavated, and within the city the presence of an earlier Roman building on the site of a church means very little. Outside the city, where Roman buildings are rare, it is of course another matter, and we have already remarked on the tendency to build churches on the sites of substantial Roman buildings, while remaining sceptical about the likelihood of a continuity of the cult. (*See pp. 136–8.*) Nevertheless, Christianity in Roman London is a historical fact, for a Bishop of London named Restitutus attended the Council of Arles in 314. He must have had a church, and if London itself continued to exist through the fifth century, as many scholars now believe, it would be surprising if all memory of it had been lost when Christianity returned and a new Bishop of London was created in 604. His new church of St Paul was built in the southern portion of an early Roman cemetery, and it seems at least possible that there was a tradition that this was sacred ground, as would have been the case if an earlier Romano-British church had been built there. The founding of such a church on the site of a marytr's shrine would be a usual development—but at present we have no more evidence for it than for the popular tradition that St Paul's was built on the site of a temple of Diana, about which Sir Christopher Wren was rightly sceptical.

There is, however, another City church with a stronger traditional claim to be of Romano-British origin. This is St Peter-upon-Cornhill, on the east wall of which is painted the proud boast: 'reputedly the oldest church site in the City, AD 179'. One might expect that such a precise date could only have been derived from documentary evidence, such as an inscription, and so it was—but the inscription was medieval. It was on a tablet that hung in the church until the seventeenth century, and stated that it was founded by 'King Lucius' in AD 179 as an Archbishop's See. In the early monkish chronicles, this Lucius is described as a British king, who invited Pope Eleutherius to send a mission for the conversion of the Britons.[1] It need hardly be said that there were no British 'kings' at this period, but there may possibly have been a clandestine mission to Britain. What is quite certain, however, is that the missionaries did *not* build a church on the site of St Peter's. In the second

---

[1] Bede: A History of the English Church and People, Penguin translation, 1955, Bk. 1, Ch. 4, p. 42.

century this was part of the great basilica, at the very heart of officialdom—and Roman officials in the reign of Marcus Aurelius were not kindly disposed towards the Christians, as is witnessed by the sufferings of the Gaulish martyrs. The medieval claim for a Roman origin for St Peter's may be based merely on the discovery there of recognizable Roman antiquities and structures—perhaps including an inscription of Lucius Verus! It is possible, however, by re-interpretation, to take a more favourable view of the tradition, and to give St Peter's the benefit of at least some doubt. There was probably an official shrine—pagan, of course—in the basilica, and, in the natural course of events, it would have been converted in the fourth century to a Christian chapel, which might still have been remembered when Christianity returned to London.

It is not impossible, therefore, that there may be some basis in historical fact for the admittedly early tradition of a Roman origin for St Peter's, and popular mythology cannot be completely disregarded without careful enquiry. Unfortunately, as London historians and archaeologists are painfully aware, in the rich historical soil of the City completely false legends can spring up overnight and, because of their appeal to local loyalties, may survive for a long time, vehemently defended by their protagonists.[1]

There may be as little basis for the claim of St Peter's as for the recent suggestion that the church of St Stephen Walbrook was built in the seventh century, 'probably on the foundations of the third century Mithras Temple'. There is no doubt about the position of the earlier church of St Stephen, which is precisely defined in Oliver's Survey of 1674, and lies some twenty yards to the north of the site of the Mithraeum.[2] We have no reason to suppose that this was not the place where the church was founded, and there was no evidence at all from the excavation to suggest that a church had ever been built on the Mithraeum. On the contrary, the presence of a medieval well cut through its south wall showed conclusively that the wall had no superstructure in the Middle Ages.

There is no need to cling to romantic myths or to invent spurious links with the past, for the truth itself is surely exciting enough, as it is revealed by the accumulation of facts which can be verified by

---

[1] In view of the recent revival of the idea in a popular booklet, it is necessary to add that there is no reason at all to suspect that St Etheldreda's Church, Ely Place, is on the site of a Roman church. The supposed 'Roman font' found there is likely to be early medieval, and may be a mortar.

[2] The position of the old church is fully discussed by S. Perks: *History of the Mansion House*, 1922, pp. 115–16.

anyone who cares to take a little trouble. Roman London was a very real place and its people still speak clearly to us across the centuries. That the present City of London has its roots in the remote past is also evident, and we shall find many more fascinating instances of this as our knowledge grows. But this knowledge must be firmly based on the solid facts produced by archaeologists and historians. The visitor who seeks the *visible* evidence in City street and cellar, and in museum show-cases, will find both objective reality and a powerful stimulus for the imagination.

Index